Total Human

The Complete Strength Training System

by

Shane Provstgaard and Craig Nybo

Illustrations by Mike Terrell

Cover photography by Scott Peterson

Additional photography by Scott Peterson and Craig Nybo

Editors: Ron Nybo, Mike Nybo

Bloomington, IN   authorHOUSE® Milton Keynes, UK

AuthorHouse™
1663 Liberty Drive, Suite 200
Bloomington, IN 47403
www.authorhouse.com
Phone: 1-800-839-8640

AuthorHouse™ UK Ltd.
500 Avebury Boulevard
Central Milton Keynes, MK9 2BE
www.authorhouse.co.uk
Phone: 08001974150

First published by AuthorHouse 10/4/2006

ISBN: 1-4259-6518-0 (sc)

Printed in the United States of America
Bloomington, Indiana

This book is printed on acid-free paper.

TABLE OF CONTENTS

MASTER CONCEPT 3: DIETING

MASTER CONCEPT 4: STAYING STRONG

CHAPTER 1: INTRODUCTION

Women do you want leaner, shaplier legs, with muscle definition? Do you want to lose the flab under your arms? Do you want shapely shoulders and tight abs? Do you want to drop a few dress sizes? Do you want to feel better and have more energy? Do I have your attention?

Men, do you want harder biceps and cut triceps? Do you want a six-pack? Do you want a chiseled lean look to your body that is sure to turn heads? Do you want a major boost in your energy and self-confidence? Do I have your attention?

The fact that you are reading this book shows that your health is a priority to you. You value your one possession that won't wear, rust, tarnish or become obsolete. You value your body. The better you treat your body, the better equipped you will be to succeed at the things in life that make you happy. After all, no matter where you go, what you do, who you meet or what you say, your body will always be with you; and if you lose your health, you lose your most valuable treasure in life.

By the end of this book, you will know your body better than ever. You will have a plan that will increase your energy and self-confidence. This plan will help you become happier and more successful than you have ever imagined. The road to personal success can be traveled much faster if you are physically fit and ready to run, not walk, down it with passion and enthusiasm.

Many training manuals teach a fitness plan, but fail to adequately explain the theory behind that plan. They don't teach the core building blocks of fitness training. This book provides a highly effective, step-by-step plan and method. It also teaches the principles behind that method by taking a scientific approach to strength training, aerobic training and dieting. If you understand the science of your body, you will be more prepared to effectively train your body and see measurable results. More importantly, you will gain confidence in the Total Human plan because it is built on a strong foundation of proven facts and truth.

The definition of knowledge is *Familiarity, awareness, or understanding gained through experience or study.* Knowledge is at the base of effective physical fitness training. The definition of wisdom is *the correct application of knowledge.* This book teaches both knowledge and wisdom as related to complete body training. Each concept is taught in 2 phases; principles (knowledge)and application of principles (wisdom).

The bottom line is that if you follow the concepts of this book, you will move toward optimum body weight while gaining valuable lean muscle mass. Lean muscle mass causes a natural and permanent boost to your body's metabolism. Every pound of lean muscle mass burns up to 50 calories per day even while one sits in a recliner and watches television.

Read on to learn how to burn more calories every day; to become stronger at an optimum rate; to look younger, more toned and more attractive. We're not talking about baby steps; we're talking about running flat-out down the road to a place where you will feel better, look better and find a goldmine of success and happiness.

So, buckle up and let's get started.

CHAPTER 2: HOW THIS BOOK WORKS

This book differs from most other training manuals; it uses a proven scientific approach to fitness training rather than unreliable opinion. Knowledge of the *science* of fitness training is essential. If you know the basic science of human physiology, you will become more confident that what you are doing will safely produce the desired results. Though the science of exercise is vast and complicated, this book teaches only the facts you need to know and presents them in easy-to-understand terms so you can train effectively without having to earn a degree in exercise science.

This book teaches 4 master concepts of effective fitness training; they are as follows:

Figure 2-1

In the application sections of the book, the header of each page is marked with a diagram like Figure 2-1, highlighted to help you quickly locate any of the four specific steps in the fitness process. Use of this guide makes it easy to flip through the pages and immediately find any part of the process you might be searching for.

Figure 2-2

The first master concept is *Body Basics* (Figure 2-2). In this section, you will learn the science of the human body. You will learn about the human muscular system. You will learn how muscles use energy, how they react to training and grow in strength and efficiency. You will also learn about the aerobic energy system. You will learn how aerobic exercise, like running and biking, helps you move towards your optimum weight while increasing energy and stamina.

TRAINING

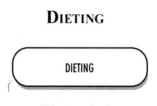

Figure 2-3

The second master concept is *Training* (Figure 2-3). In this section, you will learn advanced training principles for both weight training and cardiovascular (aerobic) training. You will learn proper lifting technique, why it is important for you to rest and recover between workouts and how to build an optimum aerobic training routine.

DIETING

Figure 2-4

The third master concept is *Dieting* (Figure 2-4). In this section of the book you will learn how your body extracts energy from food, how food is broken down and used to power everything you do. You will learn what calories are, where they come from and how your body uses them. You will learn how to calculate the number of calories you need each day to stay fit and to maintain or move towards your optimum weight.

Figure 2-5

The fourth master concept is *Staying Strong* (Figure 2-5). This section of the book is all about motivation and development of a regular maintenance routine. No physical fitness program will work without a built in method to help you stick to it. You will learn how to calculate your body fat percentage (fat to lean muscle mass ratio) and many other essential body measurements. You will learn why it is important to keep a success journal and what information should be recorded in it. This section of the book will teach you how to chart your progress.

FLOWCHART HEADERS

Each chapter header uses a flowchart, as illustrated in Figure 2-6. These charts act as roadmaps to assist you to find the location of any concept taught in the book.

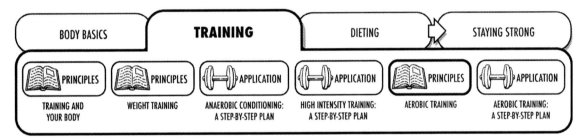

Figure 2-6

As you read the book or refer back to it later, the flow charts will also help you to know exactly where you are in the learning process. Each concept is divided into 2 phases; principles and application (Figure 2-7). First you will learn principles--why it works. Second you will learn application--how to make it work for you. This is the best way to gain a complete understanding of each powerful concept. The chapter heading icons will tell you whether you are studying principles or getting down to business in the how-to methods. Be patient. Once you get through the proper workout routine principles, you will better understand how to put the theory into practice and how to make it work for you. Just remember that step-by-step tutorials are on the way and that chapter headings will help you know where you are.

In some instances you will find that topics are repeated in both the principles and application phases of learning. This book has been written such that once you have a grasp of the principles, everything you need to execute them can be found in their respective application and tutorial sections. It is, therefore, necessary to reprint formulas and other information as a part of both learning and application of what has been taught.

Figure 2-7

By using the flowcharts at the beginning of each chapter as roadmaps, you will always know exactly where you are on the pathway to gaining a powerhouse of knowledge from this book. In the end, you will have a deep, living grasp of superior training and dieting concepts. You will be prepared to use them to achieve amazing results.

The appendix of this book contains tools to help you along the way. You will find everything you need to breathe life into what you have learned from the book. You will find a glossary of terms, in-the-gym workout sheets, exercise tutorials and blank success journal pages that you can copy and use.

CHAPTER 3: PROBLEM/SOLUTION

CHAPTER PREVIEW

Problem: obesity is the precursor to many health problems. Solution: the best weapons to use against obesity are a proper diet and exercise. This book teaches that you can have a better relationship with your body by learning its natural language.

THE PROBLEM

In this world of technology and convenience, almost anything we want is within our grasp; all we have to do is reach out for whatever we desire, whether it is food, entertainment, vacations, thrills or anything else. What we can't get for free, we pay for and it is brought to us with no effort of our own.

This phenomenon has had a negative and far reaching effect on our world-wide society. Our girth as a people is collectively growing. I'm not talking about technology, achievement, or advances in intellectual accomplishment and science; I am talking about body weight--obesity is on the rise and there seems to be no end in sight. It is exploding at a staggering rate.

The charts below show some disturbing statistics.

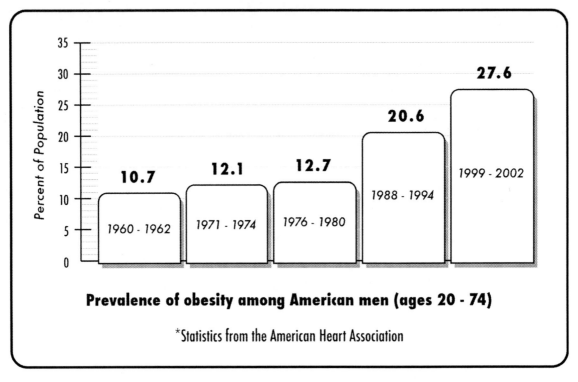

Prevalence of obesity among American men (ages 20 - 74)

*Statistics from the American Heart Association

Figure 3-1

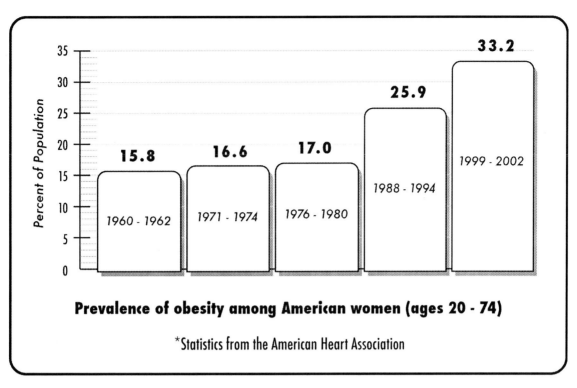

Figure 3-2

Figure 3-1 and Figure 3-2 show an exponential growth in the number of overweight and obese people in the United States. Obesity is one of the most dangerous of known health risks. Having an extra 30 pounds of body fat is the precursor to many dreadful heart and blood vessel diseases including those listed in Figure 3-3.

HEART ATTACK	STROKE	HYPERTENSION
DIABETES	ARRHYTHMIA	HIGH CHOLESTEROL
HIGH BLOOD PRESSURE	CONGESTIVE HEART FAILURE	PERIPHERAL ARTERY DISEASE

Figure 3-3

It's a tough world, and as a people we are not getting healthier. We are shortening our lives. We are shortening our time with our families and friends and the trend is not getting better.

Just like an army general must know his enemy; you must get to know yours. Your enemy is obesity. Now that you and the enemy have been properly introduced, it's time to become motivated and mobilized. Reassure yourself that you can beat this problem. You can take control. With discipline and effort, these daunting facts can become fuel for your strength and personal achievement.

THE SOLUTION

In answer to America's big weight problem, a growing number of Americans have stood up and loudly proclaimed *enough is enough!* No longer content to be members of the herd, they have chosen NOW as the time to commit to a healthy, successful and lasting future.

This call has been heard and countless get-thin-quick programs have come to cash in. There are high-carb diets, low-carb diets, gimmicks and gadgets. There are bushels of supplements and magic pills that claim big time weight loss by popping a capsule every few hours without changing your activity level. These options are often a useless waste of time and money.

You might have tried seven or eight fad diets and the same number of exercise programs, only to find you have not experienced the results promised. You might have even lost weight on one of these programs but found that the pounds just sling shot right back on within weeks of quitting.

So what is the answer to all the madness on television, in the papers and written into a whirlwind of health books? Where do you go for the real answers? The solution is easy; you go back to the basics. To find your optimum weight, look great and feel good about yourself, there are two things you have to do, maintain a **proper** diet and exercise.

Unfortunately there are thousands of **different** diet programs. Every issue of *Shape*, *Cosmopolitan*, *Reader's Digest* and other publications found on magazine racks across America tout the latest and greatest diet plan. They make unbelievable claims like, *Lose ten pounds in two weeks,* or *Eat whatever you want and still lose weight.* Be careful about such claims. Just as most get rich quick schemes are scams, most get thin quick schemes are nothing more than smoke and mirrors resulting in quick water loss and little to no actual fat loss.

With exercise, it is the same; there are countless periodicals and books written on the subject. There are thousands of variations, which in many cases conflict with one another. It's easy to get confused sifting through the gravel of information to get at the real gems.

Americans forget that *the basics* goes beyond a diet and exercise program. *The basics* delve into human physiology. If your goal is to strengthen and tone your muscles, you must understand how they work. What are your muscles doing when you lift weights? What are they doing when you go out for a run? What are they doing between workouts? How can you maximize workouts so that they can do whatever it is they do more efficiently?

What is the solution? The answer is simple--knowledge is the solution. You must know the science of your muscular system. You must know what makes up your muscles. You must know how to properly work the muscles of your body and how to achieve maximum performance.

You might be thinking, *whoa, please don't turn this into biology 101.* Don't worry; the intent of this book is to explain everything you need to know in the simplest terms possible to allow you to achieve the shapely, fat burning body that you want.

As a human being you have five senses; sight, smell, hearing, taste and touch. Let's add a new sense to that list, the sense of self--the sense of *yourself.* With this book, you will learn to listen to your body's language. You will learn to understand your body's valuable feedback and have the ability to adapt your training program based on what your body tells you.

At the end of this book, you will know yourself muscle-by-muscle, tendon-by-tendon and breath-by-breath. That knowledge is power--power in you like a diesel engine. With that kind of power under the hood, you can turn the key and experience a wonderful change in your life; a transformation into something truly beautiful--a better, more gratifying you.

INTRODUCING YOU TO YOU

The greatest pleasures in life come from relationships--relationships with your spouse, your parents, your friends, your relatives and your co-workers. Though relationships usually have meager beginnings, they can be fostered into long-lasting friendships with care and frequent contact. As relationships evolve, you discover traits about others that you like; you also discover traits that you don't care for. You learn to weigh the pros and cons of relationships, recognizing which parts are pleasing and which are painful.

Just like fostering a relationship with another person, you can foster a relationship with yourself--a relationship between you and your body. The rules of this type of relationship are about the same as those of a relationship between you and another person. The relationship between you and your body can be strengthened by learning to read your body's *language* and by responding to what your body tells you by giving it exactly what it needs to improve itself.

So without further delay, let's make the introduction.

I'd like to introduce YOU to YOU.

CHAPTER SUMMARY

PROBLEM/SOLUTION

- Problem: obesity is rising at a staggering rate.
- Problem: many serious illness begin with obesity.
- Problem: there are many dieting and exercise plans out there.
- Solution: a proper dieting and exercise program is the best way to better your health.
- Solution: This book teaches a proper dieting and exercise program that is based on science.
- Solution: This book teaches that you can have a better relationship with your body by learning your body's natural language and fulfilling its needs.

MASTER CONCEPT 1: BODY BASICS

- How your muscular system works
- Your 12 major muscle groups defined
- How your muscles spend energy
- How your anaerobic energy system works
- How your aerobic system works

CHAPTER 4: HOW YOUR MUSCLES WORK

PRINCIPLES

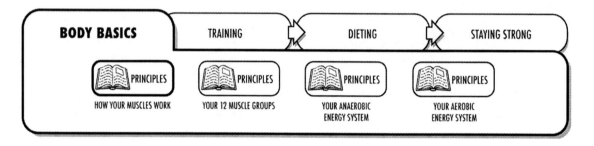

| BODY BASICS | TRAINING | DIETING | STAYING STRONG |

PRINCIPLES — HOW YOUR MUSCLES WORK

PRINCIPLES — YOUR 12 MUSCLE GROUPS

PRINCIPLES — YOUR ANAEROBIC ENERGY SYSTEM

PRINCIPLES — YOUR AEROBIC ENERGY SYSTEM

CHAPTER PREVIEW

There are 3 types of muscle types; skeletal muscle, smooth muscle and cardiac muscle. Muscles can only contract. Muscles are arranged for optimal movement of joints. Muscles are made up of muscle fibers. There are 3 types of muscle fibers; each acts differently when stressed.

YOUR THREE MUSCLE TYPES

Muscles are often taken for granted. They perform their assigned tasks without your ever having to think about them. They are the workhorses of your body. Walking, running, standing up, sitting down, blinking, and all other motion is performed by your muscles.

Muscles are like an automobile engine. An engine uses energy in the form of gasoline and converts it into motion. Muscles take energy, with carbohydrates and protein as fuels, and converts it into motion.

There are three types of muscles in your body.

First, there are skeletal muscles. These muscles are attached to your skeleton. Their function is to make you move--such as the bending of your elbows and knees. Skeletal muscles are controlled voluntarily, which means they receive their orders to move at will through your central nervous system.

Second, there are smooth muscles. These muscles are found in your digestive system, blood vessels and bladder. Smooth muscles have the ability to remain contracted over long periods of time. Smooth muscles act involuntary, meaning they work on their own. You don't have to think about using smooth muscles for them to function. How monotonous would life be if you had to think about digesting food all day long? You probably wouldn't get anything else done.

Cardiac muscles are the third category. These muscles are found exclusively in the heart. Their main properties are toughness and consistency. Cardiac muscles can stretch like smooth muscles and contract like skeletal muscles. Like smooth muscles, cardiac muscles work involuntarily.

Skeletal muscles are the main muscles of concern when it comes to weight training. These muscles are arranged ingeniously throughout your body--attached to your bones by tendons. Their purpose is to move your body efficiently and smoothly.

MUSCLES CONTRACT

Muscles can only contract and relax; they do not have the ability to forcefully expand. The stronger your muscles are able to contract, the stronger you are.

Think of your elbow, one of the many joints in your body. Your elbow works like a hinge. Muscles are attached by tendons to your bones on the inside and outside of your elbow. If you want to bend your elbow, your brain sends a signal through your nervous system to the muscles on the inside of your elbow, telling them to contract. The muscles on the inside of your elbow then contract, pulling your elbow joint closed. To open your elbow, your brain sends a signal through your nervous system, telling the muscles on the outside of your elbow to contract and simultaneously telling the muscles of your inner elbow to relax. Your muscles obey and your elbow joint opens up.

The contracting force of muscles can be strengthened by adding resistance. When a muscle experiences resistance to its ability to contract, it will grow stronger in order to adapt to the added resistance. Weight lifting is the best way to add resistance. If you bend your elbow with no added weight, the muscles on the inside of your arm concern themselves with lifting the weight of your forearm and hand only; with no added resistance, muscle contraction is a simple task.

However, if you hold a heavy dumbbell (resistance) and try the same motion, the muscles on the inside of your elbow will have a more difficult time contracting and must adapt and strengthen to meet the challenge. Resistance training, or weight training, is the act of lifting weight to increase the contraction force of your muscles.

ALL MUSCLES ARE NOT CREATED EQUALLY

Muscles are made up of bundles of cells called muscle fibers. You can think of muscle fibers as groups of bundled cables running in the same direction. For the purpose of strength training there are three types of muscle fibers, slow twitch, medium twitch and fast twitch muscle fibers. Each muscle is made up of groupings of all 3 fiber types. Each fiber type performs differently.

Slow twitch muscle fibers can contract against lower levels of resistance or lift smaller amounts of weight for longer, sustained periods of time before muscle failure (the point at which muscles fatigue to a state where they can no longer hold the weight and must relax).

Fast twitch fibers can contract against higher levels of resistance (more weight) but fail quicker than slow twitch muscles. Fast twitch muscle fibers are called into play when higher amounts of weight or resistance are lifted.

Medium twitch fibers, of which there are two types, are somewhere between fast twitch and slow twitch in their abilities.

When performing a task such as lifting a heavy weight, each fiber type is called upon by your central nervous system in logical order; this is called *the principle of orderly recruitment.*

The order in which muscle fiber types are recruited depends on the intensity of the task muscles are called upon to perform. Tasks can range from simple and mundane, like washing a car or vacuuming a rug (low intensity), to complicated and extreme, like flat-out sprinting, competition swimming or weight lifting (high intensity).

By *orderly recruitment*, the minimum amount of muscle fibers are used by the body to handle any task. Muscle fiber types are called to act in logical order. Like water, your muscles choose the path of least resistance, using only the required muscles to perform every-day tasks and saving the big guns for rare, intense bursts of energy.

Slow twitch muscle fibers are your day-to-day muscle fibers. They are used exclusively for most everything you do. They are the first muscle fibers called on to perform any task. Activities like walking a dog, washing a car or cleaning house are low intensity tasks-- perfectly suited for slow twitch muscle fibers.

Low intensity tasks can be performed for long periods of time. One Saturday you might spend the morning mowing the lawn, take two hours to wash and detail the car and finish up by cleaning the house. Once the house is clean, you might putter in the garage or go for a walk. Slow twitch muscle fibers keep you moving all day long, doing these low intensity tasks.

For medium intensity tasks, the bigger guns or medium twitch muscle fibers are called into play. Moderate weight lifting or jogging requires more force than day-to-day activities like walking a dog or washing a car, thus medium twitch muscle fibers are called into action for these kinds of tasks.

Medium intensity tasks cannot be performed for extended periods of time without a rest or a reduction in intensity because medium twitch muscle fibers reach an exhaustion point sooner than slow twitch muscle fibers. Yard work of moderate intensity like raking leaves is perfectly suited for medium twitch muscle fibers. After an extended period of time raking leaves, the medium twitch muscle fibers in the arms exhaust their energy. Once the energy is spent, the rake has to be put down for a while to allow medium twitch fibers time to recover.

For high intensity tasks the really big guns, or fast twitch muscle fibers, are called into play. These are your emergency muscles. They are meant to get you out of sticky jams. If you have to run from a frothing grizzly bear in the forest, your fast twitch muscle fibers are your best friend. Fast twitch muscle fibers are rarely used day to day, but when you need them, they are there to jump to your rescue.

Flat-out sprinting and heavy-duty weight lifting are examples of high intensity tasks that require fast twitch muscle fibers. Fast twitch fibers can contract against higher levels of resistance than medium twitch fibers but expire sooner. Bursts of extreme force can last only seconds. The human body cannot sprint at top speed for miles. A notable characteristic of fast twitch muscle fibers is that they have the greatest potential for growth; though all fibers adapt to a higher level of performance due to forced contraction at high intensity.

Effective weight training involves the recruitment of all three muscle fiber types at the same time. For maximum results, the intensity of exercise must be at a level where fast, medium and slow twitch muscle fiber types all work together and exhaust as much energy as possible.

CHAPTER SUMMARY

HOW YOUR MUSCLES WORK

- There are three types of muscles in the human body.
  - o Skeletal
  - o Smooth
  - o Cardiac
- Muscles can only contract. They cannot forcefully expand.
- Muscles are strengthened by contracting against added resistance (weight).
- Muscles are made up of three fiber types.
  - o Slow twitch muscle fibers for everyday tasks
  - o Medium twitch muscle fibers for mid-intensity tasks
  - o Fast twitch muscle fibers for high intensity tasks
- Muscle failure is the point at which muscles expire, having spent all of their immediate energy.
- Effective strength training involves working all three muscle fiber types simultaneously, with an emphasis on fast twitch fiber, and exhausting as much muscle energy as possible.

CHAPTER 5: YOUR TWELVE MUSCLE GROUPS

PRINCIPLES

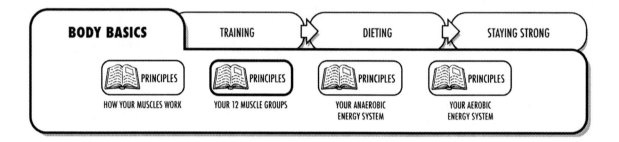

CHAPTER PREVIEW

The human body is divided into 12 muscle groups. Each group is made up of primary muscles and smaller, helper muscles.

Twelve Parts Make a Whole

A muscle is like a single elastic band with the ability to contract when willed to do so; groups of these single bands work together to accomplish a set of complicated movements. To insure that your elbow bends at exactly the right angle it is necessary to use groups of single muscles, each group contracting from the right point with the correct tension. Larger groups of these subgroups make up what are called muscle groups.

Muscle groups are large areas of the muscular system that work in symmetry to perform a set of tasks. Examples of muscle groups are the upper back muscle group and the chest muscle group. Each group has many sets of muscles that are attached to the skeleton and aligned to contract in different directions. By working together, muscles in any muscle group can accomplish exact and optimal movement of the human body.

Some weight training exercises are designed to work entire muscle groups. If these exercises are executed with perfect form, the maximum number of muscles within the worked group will contract as completely and effectively as possible.

The human body has 12 major muscle groups. Figure 5-1 thru Figure 5-4 describe all 12 groups. These figures do not represent a comprehensive list of every muscle in the entire human body; that would take several pages. We are only concerned with major muscle groups and helper muscle groups within the larger groups as they pertain to strength training and body building.

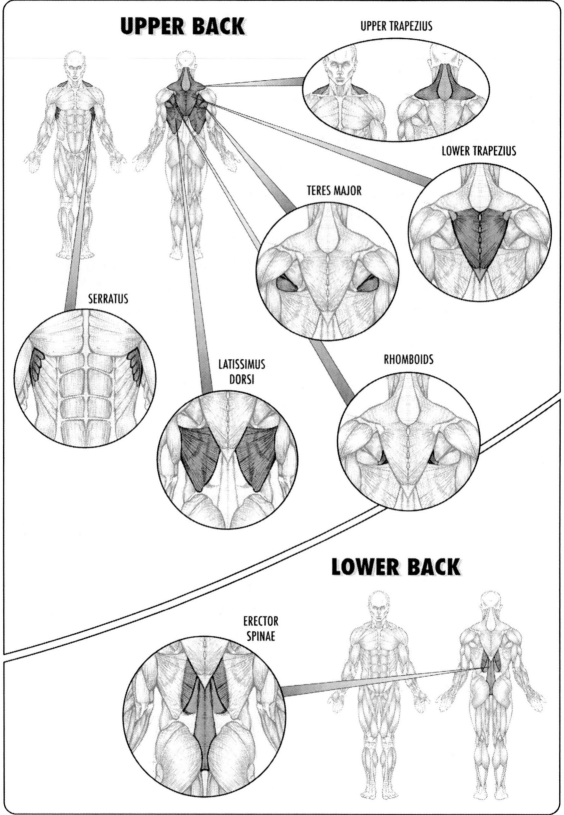

Figure 5-1

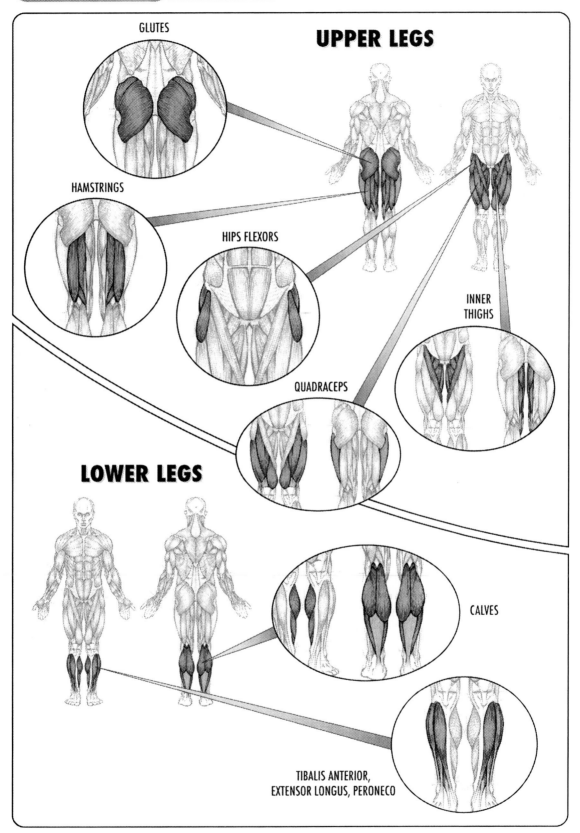

GLUTES

UPPER LEGS

HAMSTRINGS

HIPS FLEXORS

INNER THIGHS

QUADRACEPS

LOWER LEGS

CALVES

TIBALIS ANTERIOR,
EXTENSOR LONGUS, PERONECO

Figure 5-2

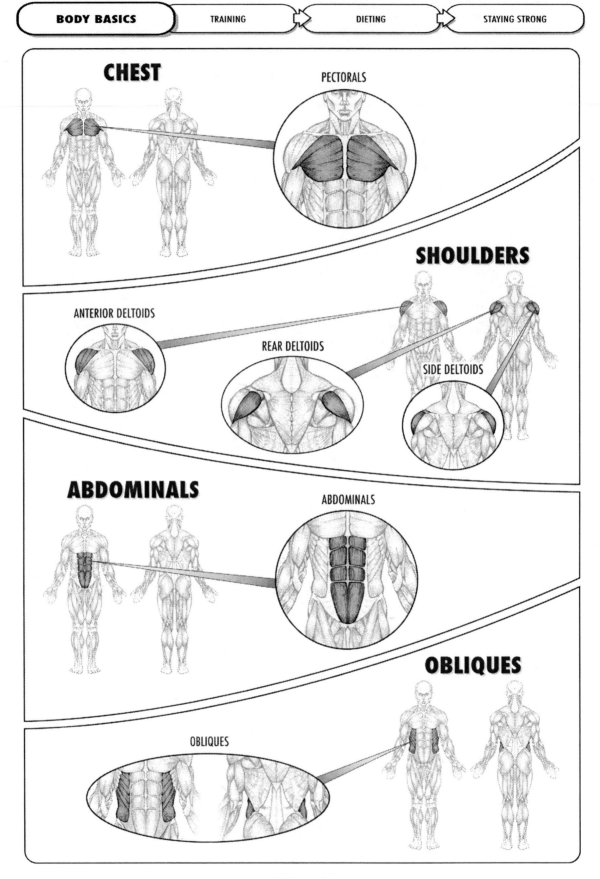

Figure 5-3

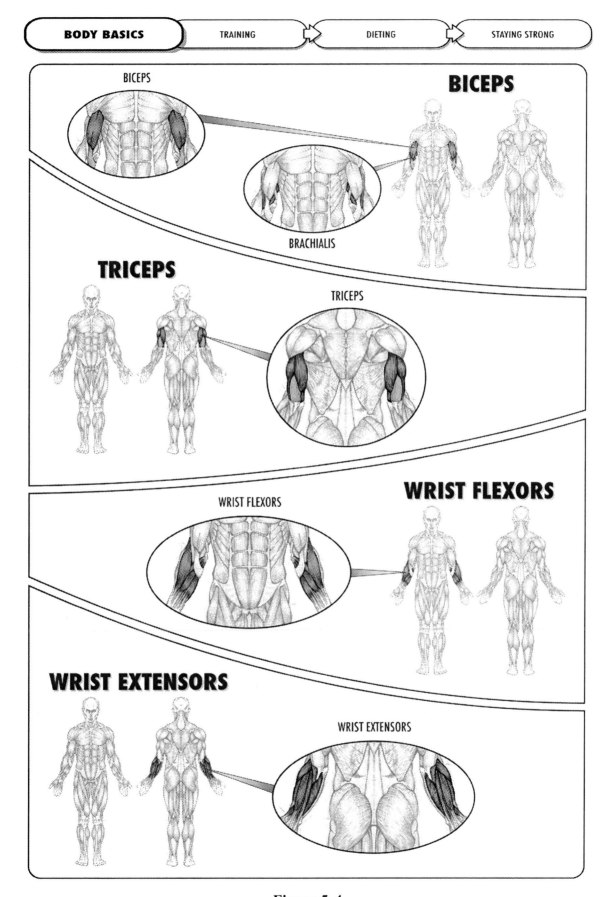

Figure 5-4

Chapter Summary

Principles: Your Twelve Muscle Groups

- Muscle groups are groupings of single muscles and smaller groups of single muscles that all work together to accomplish specific sets of tasks.
- The human muscular system is divided into 12 muscle groups.
- The most efficient exercises are designed to simultaniously work as many single muscles as possible within a muscle group.

CHAPTER 6: YOUR ANAEROBIC ENERGY SYSTEM

PRINCIPLES

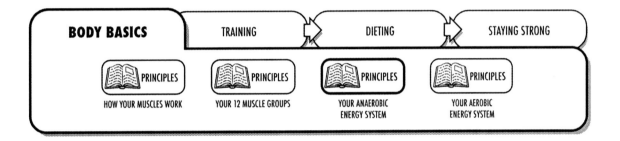

BODY BASICS	TRAINING	DIETING	STAYING STRONG
PRINCIPLES	PRINCIPLES	PRINCIPLES	PRINCIPLES
HOW YOUR MUSCLES WORK	YOUR 12 MUSCLE GROUPS	YOUR ANAEROBIC ENERGY SYSTEM	YOUR AEROBIC ENERGY SYSTEM

CHAPTER PREVIEW

The anaerobic energy system creates motion by using stored fuel in the muscles. Oxygen and fat are not used as a fuel source for the anaerobic energy system. This system is used for high-intensity activities like lifting heavy weight. High intensity activities exhaust the anaerobic energy system's fuel in a short time period.

ENERGY EQUALS MOTION

Exercise can be broken into two separate categories, aerobic exercise and anaerobic exercise. Your body reacts and adapts differently to each of these exercise categories.

The difference between these two categories of exercise is in how muscular energy is spent. Anaerobic means energy spent without the use of oxygen. Aerobic means energy spent with the use of oxygen.

ANAEROBIC ENERGY SYSTEM

You have a powerful energy system in your body called the anaerobic energy system. Anaerobic exercise is defined as high intensity, short duration exercise like weight lifting. This type of exercise relies on the anaerobic energy system because the anaerobic energy system stores a potent but limited amount of energy that can be called on immediately. The anaerobic system is able to spend its energy freely and instantaneously because it does not use oxygen as an ingredient to produce energy. The anaerobic energy system is broken down into two sub-systems; the ATP-Pc system and the glycolytic energy system.

THE ATP-Pc ENERGY SYSTEM

The ATP-Pc system burns units of fast available energy stored in your muscles without the use of oxygen. You can think of this stored energy as little specs of flash powder that, when ignited, are burned immediately--explosive and powerful. When you lift a weight or engage in any kind of intense muscular action, energy in your ATP-Pc system is quickly spent and must be replenished.

The flash powder specs in the analogy are actually limited amounts of ready energy called ATP, which is stored in your muscles. ATP is a powerhouse of fast energy that your body can draw on at a moment's notice. Because ATP does not require the use of oxygen, it is spent quickly and is used for high intensity, low duration activities such as weight training and sprinting.

The ATP-Pc system spends its entire supply of ATP within the first 10 seconds of intense muscular action. After that 10-second power-burst of energy, the ATP-Pc system must be reloaded with fresh ATP.

When the ATP-Pc system is spent, the second anaerobic sub-system, or glycolytic energy system, takes over. The transition is like a relay race. The baton in the race symbolizes heavy muscular activity. When you begin a set of heavy exercise, like the bench press, the ATP-Pc system kicks in, turning ready stored energy (ATP) into motion. This gives you the power to perform the exercise. After about 10 seconds of heavy lifting, the baton is passed from the ATP-Pc system to the glycolytic energy system and the race continues. Your body performs the transition from system to system without a hitch.

THE GLYCOLYTIC ENERGY SYSTEM

Just as a car needs fuel to run in the form of gasoline, your muscles need fuel to run in the form of ATP. When a car's gas tank runs dry, it must be refilled with gasoline to keep the car running. Your glycolytic energy system is the mechanism that refills your muscles with fuel by creating ATP for your muscles to burn.

Gasoline is created by refining crude oil into a fine, combustible liquid that can be burned by an automobile engine. Your glycolytic energy system acts as a sort of refinery, but instead of crude oil, it uses a raw ingredient called glycogen. Glycogen is a stored carbohydrate in your body--crude energy ready to be refined into fuel that can be burned by your muscles to create motion.

Your glycolytic energy system breaks glycogen down into glucose. Glucose is a sugar that circulates in your blood--the major energy source for the human body. Glucose is broken down to produce ATP. Once ATP is loaded in the muscles, boom, the powerhouse has been turned back on and you can resume bench pressing that barbell.

During the breakdown of glycogen, a by-product called lactic acid is produced. Lactic acid is thought to cause the burning sensation in your muscles while lifting heavy weights. When the buildup of lactic acid hits a certain threshold, the muscle contraction process is short-circuited and you have to stop exercising and take a break. Lactic acid is thought of as one of the major reasons for muscle failure.

The glycolytic energy system spends its energy supply in under 2 minutes of sustained intense muscular contraction (lifting of heavy weight).

Back to the relay race example. The ATP-Pc system picks up the baton, runs as hard as it can for 10 seconds and hands it off to the glycolytic energy system. The glycolytic energy system runs for roughly a minute and 50 seconds and collapses over the finish line with no more energy to spend. Both anaerobic subsystems exhaust their supply of energy in about 120 seconds (as illustrated in Figure 6-1).

Figure 6-1

TRAINING THE ANAEROBIC ENERGY SYSTEM

When the anaerobic energy system is regularly trained, the body adapts by adding pounds of lean muscle mass to more efficiently handle short bursts of intense physical activity. The type of training activity doesn't matter; muscles don't distinguish between swinging a sledgehammer, running from wolves or lifting a barbell; all are high intensity activities. If the body is subject to any of them on a consistent basis, it must adapt.

One of the most exciting benefits of putting on lean muscle mass is found in muscle tissue's ability to burn away extra calories. Muscles require energy to function. Every one pound of lean muscle mass uses up to fifty calories each day to stay primed. That energy comes from your fat fuel reserves. The more lean muscle you have, the more energy your body requires; hence, the more calories are burned. The best way to burn away fat is to pack on as much lean muscle mass as you can.

Men tend to bulk up--muscles grow, harden and stand out. The ripped look comes from a natural loss of body fat, which occurs as the result of consistent anaerobic workouts and dieting. Guys, with anaerobic training, you can expect bigger, harder biceps and triceps; you can expect hard, shapely pecs and a nice six-pack. Sound good?

Without the use of steroids, women don't bulk up like men. Women tend to drop body fat and tone up without putting on a lot of mass like men. Women, with anaerobic training you can expect definition in your body, toner legs and shoulders, tighter buns and a shapely stomach. Sound good? Keep reading.

CHAPTER SUMMARY

PRINCIPLES: YOUR ANAEROBIC ENERGY SYSTEM

- Anaerobic exercise does not use oxygen and fat as fuels.
- ATP is a form of fuel stored in the muscles that is used to power the anaerobic energy system.
- The two subsystems of the anaerobic energy system are the ATP-Pc energy system and the glycolytic energy system.
- The ATP-Pc energy system burns its entire store of fuel (ATP) after about 10 seconds of high intensity muscular activity.
- The glycolytic energy system takes over when the ATP-Pc energy system runs out of fuel.
- The glycolytic energy system produces ATP and loads the muscles to sustain high intensity activities.
- Lactic acid is a byproduct of the glycolytic energy system and is thought to cause the burning sensation in the muscles while lifting weights.
- The anaerobic energy system, including both of its sub-systems, burns its supply of fuel (ATP) after about 110 to 120 seconds of high intensity muscular activity.
- If the anaerobic energy system is trained with high intensity activity on a regular basis, it is forced to adapt by building new muscle mass.
- Lean muscle mass causes the body to increase the calorie burn rate, which results in body fat reduction.

CHAPTER 7: YOUR AEROBIC ENERGY SYSTEM

PRINCIPLES

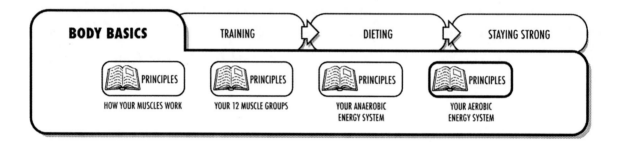

CHAPTER PREVIEW

The aerobic system uses fat and oxygen as fuels to create motion. This system is used for lower intensity activities over longer time periods.

OXYGEN EQUALS POWER

The aerobic or oxidative energy system requires the use of oxygen to produce energy. This energy system is best suited for long duration, low intensity activities like marathon running or walking. Oxygen and fat are used as fuels by the aerobic energy system to sustain motion over extended periods of time.

Using the relay race example; the aerobic or oxidative energy system sees the anaerobic energy system collapse over its finish line. It takes the baton out of the anaerobic system's quivering hand and continues fueling the muscles, this time using oxygen and fat as fuels to produce motion.

The baton pass is not transparent this time because aerobic energy system doesn't have the same explosive power as the anaerobic system. Once the anaerobic system has spent its energy, the weights must be put down or the sprinter must stop sprinting and take a rest.

But what the aerobic energy system lacks in power, it makes up for in endurance. Mid to low intensity tasks can be performed for long periods of time, even for hours depending on the intensity of the activity.

TRAINING THE AEROBIC ENERGY SYSTEM

The body adapts differently with aerobic training than with anaerobic training. Aerobic exercises are extended, mid to low intensity activities that do not fully tax the anaerobic energy system; running and walking long distances are good examples. Consistent training of the aerobic energy system forces the body to adapt; but the body adapts differently than with anaerobic training. Bulky muscle mass is kept to a minimum. The body seeks to be nimble and light in order to sustain mid to low intensity activities over long periods of time. With oxygen and fats used as fuels, the heart becomes a big player in sustaining mid to low aerobic activities. The heart works hard to pump oxygen and fat into the blood stream to be used as energy ingredients. With consistent training of the aerobic energy system, the heart adapts by becoming stronger.

Aerobic training trims the body down and increases aerobic efficiency. Champion marathon runners have a slim and sleek look to them. This is evidence of continuously working the aerobic system over extended periods of time with little exercise of the anaerobic system.

The benefits of any training regimen come from the effects of the body's ability to adapt and improve its performance. To force adaptation of either the anaerobic or aerobic energy system, you must push beyond your daily normal activity level; you must exercise.

If your goal is to lose pounds fast and tone up, a good balance of aerobic and anaerobic exercise is the best approach.

Chapter Summary

Principles

Your Aerobic Energy System

- The aerobic energy system is used for mid to low intensity activities over long periods of time.
- The aerobic energy system uses oxygen and fat as ingredients for fuel.
- Training the aerobic energy system trims the body down and strengthens the heart.
- A good balance of aerobic and anaerobic exercise is the best way to loose fat and tone up.

MASTER CONCEPT 2: TRAINING

| BODY BASICS | TRAINING | DIETING | STAYING STRONG |

- An introduction to *High Intensity Training*
- Energy debt and metabolic after-burn
- The four bedrock principles of weight training
- Weight lifting technique
- Rest and recovery
- Training fallacies

CHAPTER 8: TRAINING AND YOUR BODY

PRINCIPLES

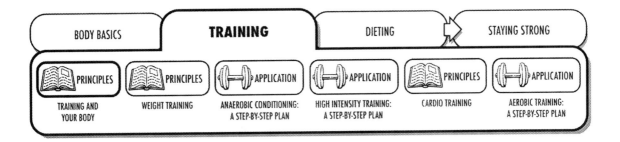

| BODY BASICS | **TRAINING** | DIETING | STAYING STRONG |

| PRINCIPLES | PRINCIPLES | APPLICATION | APPLICATION | PRINCIPLES | APPLICATION |
| TRAINING AND YOUR BODY | WEIGHT TRAINING | ANAEROBIC CONDITIONING: A STEP-BY-STEP PLAN | HIGH INTENSITY TRAINING: A STEP-BY-STEP PLAN | CARDIO TRAINING | AEROBIC TRAINING: A STEP-BY-STEP PLAN |

CHAPTER PREVIEW

High Intensity Training is the most effective weight training style. Energy is spent while working out, muscle growth occurs during rest and recovery time between workouts. There is an increase in metabolism for hours to days after working out.

HIGH INTENSITY TRAINING

The most efficient method of strength training is the HIT (High Intensity Training) method. When you hear the words *high intensity training*, you might imagine professional body builders with three percent body fat and over 200 pounds of muscle, hard as rocks.

Don't be intimidated; high intensity training is for everyone. It is the absolute best way to get the quickest toning and trimming results possible. Imagine HIT training as a way to cut through the nonsense and get right down to the brass tacks of building your body. It's a way to make every minute in the gym productive and every day of recovery count.

For a better understanding of HIT training, let's break down the acronym a letter at a time.

<u>H</u>igh – This word in the context of HIT training stands for the maximum level of muscular work a person can safely achieve.

<u>I</u>ntensity – Intensity is the level of exhaustion muscles reach during a period of time exercising (lifting weights).

<u>T</u>raining - Training is the process of working the muscles by utilizing the anaerobic and/or aerobic systems harder than they usually work to force adaptation to a new higher level.

Proper HIT training works better than any other strength training method because it is highly personalized to your specific body profile. Each of your muscle groups are not created equally. One-size-fits-all training systems are not the way to go. What works for someone else might not work for you. To simply prescribe three sets of 100-pound bench presses for all does not meet everyone's immediate needs. Your muscular system makeup is different than anyone else's. Your muscles adapt differently than anyone else's. Customized HIT training helps you listen to your body's feedback and prescribe just the right amount of lifting time, weight and recovery for each of your muscle groups. With HIT, you act as the personal trainer for each of your muscle groups individually.

BURN CALORIES WHILE YOU WATCH TV

How would you like to burn extra calories while sitting at your desk, watching television or just plain old lounging around? I have good news; this can be done. It's called metabolic after-burn and it's one of the greatest advantages of high intensity training.

To function, your body must have an adequate supply of energy. When you workout, you drain your body's energy reserves and your body is left in a state of energy debt.

Once your body is drained, it has no choice; it must pay back that energy debt by restoring the lost energy. This process is called metabolic after-burn and, if you are trying to lose weight, it is truly your friend.

ENERGY DEBT

During workouts, the body uses up its supply of the essential energy ingredient, glycogen. The muscles also sustain a small amount of controlled damage. This is a natural step in muscle adaptation and growth. The combination of energy loss and muscle damage temporarily weakens the body's ability to move and function normally. This weakening is called inroading. Inroading is a level of fatigue that temporarily incapacitates the muscles. You might feel stiff and sore for a day or two after a heavy workout. The stiffness and pain is the result of inroading. You have stressed your muscles and your body needs to adapt to this stress by rebuilding and replenishing energy reserves.

To recover from inroading, your body needs energy in the form of calories. To get those essential calories, your body raises its metabolic rate for several hours to days, taking the calories from fat reserves and nutrients you put into your body. Research shows a heightened metabolic rate of 5% or higher for several hours following high intensity anaerobic training. A higher metabolic rate means more calories burned long after you have finished training.

How many extra calories do you burn? Let's say Steve, a 140-pound man, 29 years old, burns 1,680 calories per day at rest. With a 5% increase to his metabolic rate, he burns an extra 84 calories per day at rest--about the same amount of calories he would burn while running a 10-minute mile. The exciting thing is that those 84 calories are burned no matter what Steve does. Let's say Steve spends half the day watching sitcom reruns and follows up with a nice nap in a recliner. He has still burned 84 extra calories while recovering from inroading.

Your metabolism continues to work out, burning extra calories long after you leave the gym. You are actually burning away body fat without even thinking about it. This is an exciting benefit of high intensity training.

CHAPTER SUMMARY

PRINCIPLES

TRAINING AND YOUR BODY

- High intensity training is the best form of anaerobic training because it is customized to your body's muscular makeup.
- Inroading is a temporary state of muscular incapacitation caused by high-intensity activity such as lifting weights.
- Working out causes energy debt. The energy must be paid back during rest and recovery periods.
- Metabolism quickens by 5% or more for hours to days after working out while the body restores its energy to the muscle system. Even at rest, extra calories are burned during the recovery process. The additional calories burned can result in reduced body fat.

CHAPTER 9: WEIGHT TRAINING

PRINCIPLES

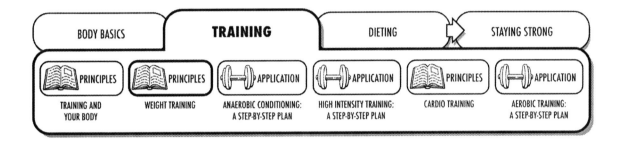

CHAPTER PREVIEW

Anaerobic training is broken into 4 bedrock principles; volume, intensity, duration and frequency. For maximum results, correct volume is determined by the intensity of exercise. A proper warm-up and cool-down are necessary parts of any workout. Large muscle groups should be worked first during a workout. Slow and even movement should be used to perform any weight lifting exercise. Flexibility training should be performed at the end of a weight training session. Complete recovery between workouts is essential. Weight training fallacies should be known and avoided.

WEIGHT TRAINING BASICS

Weight training can be broken into the following four components: volume, duration, frequency and intensity. A thorough understanding of each component is needed to help you most effectively use your time in the gym or in your home gym and to guarantee optimum results.

VOLUME

Volume is the amount of work muscles do in a unit of time. In strength training, volume is measured in the following three ways: The number of repetitions, the number of sets and the amount of time spent performing each exercise.

A repetition or rep is the act of performing one complete exercise. One bench press, one dumbbell curl or one leg extension each equal one rep.

Sets are groups of reps. You might perform a set of 10 reps of bench presses or a set of 5 reps of bicep curls.

The third, and possibly most important measurement of volume, is the amount of time spent performing an exercise. *Time under load* (TUL) is an important term to remember. During a set of exercise the working muscles are said to be *under load*. If you pick up a pair of dumbbells to perform a set of dumbbell curls, the instant you begin the dumbbell curl motion, your biceps are *under load*. The amount of time from the moment you begin the first dumbbell curl to the end of the last dumbbell curl is said to be your *time under load.*

Volume and intensity are inversely related; the higher the volume, the lower the intensity and visa versa. You can either lift 5 pounds 100 times over 10 minutes time--that's high volume training; or you can lift 100 pounds 10 times over 90 seconds--that's high intensity training. For the best results, your goal should be to train with high intensity rather than with high volume. This book will teach you how.

INTENSITY

As weight is increased for a set of exercise during a specified period of time, more energy is required for the muscles expend; the muscles get closer to exhaustion and the intensity of the exercise is increased.

The level of exhaustion the muscles reach during exercise is the direct result of intensity. If you bicep curl a small weight, perhaps a 5-pound dumbbell, for 25 seconds with slow controlled motion, you would probably not come very close to exhausting the muscles of your bicep; thus, the intensity of this exercise is classified as low.

If you perform the same bicep curl with a 30-pound dumbbell over the same 25 seconds with slow, controlled motion, exhaustion in your bicep muscles will be more profound. If your bicep reaches muscle failure before finishing one full 25-second set and you are forced to stop and take a rest, the intensity of this exercise is considered high.

DURATION

Duration is the amount of time you spend in the gym. Duration is inversely related to intensity; the longer the duration, the less the intensity and visa versa. Duration is also related to volume; the longer the duration, the higher the volume.

Duration includes time performing exercises as well as rest time between sets. Clocked rest times help optimize duration. Each rest time between sets should be no longer than 2 minutes.

Distractions in the gym are a quick way to decrease the effectiveness of a workout. One reason to join a gym is to socialize. Let's face it; going to the gym is a great way to meet other people, whether it is an attractive member of the opposite sex or a long lost friend. Many visit the gym in groups, gabbing and talking the whole time and paying only cursory attention to their workouts. Stopping between sets of exercise to talk about the stock market, the daily news or to engage in a pleasant conversation adds to the duration of a workout and greatly reduces intensity.

Time in the gym should be invested wisely, whether lifting or resting. Once a workout begins, the clock is ticking; use the time judiciously.

FREQUENCY

Frequency is the fourth and final component of effective exercise. Frequency is how often one works out.

Muscle growth doesn't happen during workouts. It happens during recovery time between gym visits. Muscles are like good soldiers, when they receive the order to lift, they put every ounce of energy they have into following that order. They lift until every last ounce of strength is gone. Muscles can't discern whether a workout is in an air-conditioned gym or in a life-threatening situation. They simply follow their marching orders as they are received through the central nervous system. Once the energy is gone, muscles have to stop; this is called muscle failure. Muscle failure is not a bad thing during a workout. In fact, muscle failure should be your goal whenever you perform a set of weight lifting exercise.

Once muscles are exhausted, your body immediately goes into recovery mode. When fully recovered, the muscles come back stronger, bigger and better able to handle future high intensity workouts. In the process, calories are burned, shaping and toning of muscles occurs and new, lean muscle mass is built.

Frequency is inversely related to intensity. If workouts are intense and hard hitting--expiring a high number of muscle fibers--it takes longer to fully recover. More recovery days between workouts means less frequent visits to the gym.

Required resting time for full recovery varies from person to person. The important thing is that the body must recover fully between workouts.

DETERMINING CORRECT VOLUME

The ability to determine the proper volume of exercise for each muscle group is at the center of any good workout regimen.

Volume relates to the number of sets performed of any exercise. Volume is the quantity of exercise performed or the actual time spent performing an exercise. It is possible to achieve maximum intensity (muscle work) with very little volume. If you bench press 300 pounds and hit muscular failure at 20 seconds, you would only have 20 seconds of volume; but man, weren't those 20 seconds intense?!

Using general amounts of volume, such as 10 sets of 10 bench presses three times a week, is not the most effective method. It is best to allow intensity to dictate volume.

Two criteria must be met during a set of exercise to guarantee that muscles are properly worked.

First, a maximum amount of muscle fiber must be exhausted. Exercise must be intense enough to call on all three muscle fiber types, fast, medium and slow twitch.

Second, the anaerobic energy system must be worked primarily. Since the anaerobic system exhausts its energy in the first 2 minutes of intense exercise, muscle failure must be hit within that 2 minutes (1 minute is better in both cases); otherwise, the baton is passed to the aerobic system and the exercise becomes useless as a means to increase muscle mass.

To insure that both of these objectives are met, your goal should be to hit total muscle failure within 45 to 60 seconds when performing any weight training exercise.

Volume should be consistent; you should strive to hit muscle failure within the same time frame with every exercise. Weight is not a constant; it changes over time as muscles grow and adapt. To hit muscle failure between 45 and 60 seconds, you might have to increase or decrease the weight on the bar. The first time you perform a set of bench presses, you might hit muscle failure at 50 seconds while lifting 150 pounds. After your muscles grow and adapt, it might take 170 pounds to hit muscle failure in the same 45 to 60 seconds.

By lifting enough weight to hit muscle failure, you can be sure that all three muscle fiber types are being worked. By hitting muscle failure between 45 and 60 seconds, you can be positive that the vast majority of work is done by your anaerobic energy system and not your aerobic energy system.

Muscle failure is a must. True muscle failure means every ounce of energy in the muscles is spent and the muscles are forced to stop. To hit true muscle failure, you must endure through the muscle burn and hard work of lifting and spend every last ounce of energy. Don't lift until your muscles merely burn; lift until your muscles have to call it quits because they just don't have the punch to move the weight another millimeter, then with perfect form, try one more rep.

Let's look at an example. Jane, a physically fit woman, gets ready to perform a set of bench presses. She racks up 135 pounds. She lies back on the bench and starts her stopwatch. A spotter helps her lift the bar from the forks. Using a slow, deliberate pace, she begins a set of bench presses. In the middle of the fourth rep, the muscles of her chest fail; she can't lift the bar another inch. Jane's spotter helps her re-rack the weight. She stops her stopwatch and sees that her total time performing the exercise (time under load) is 53 seconds--between 45 and 60 seconds--right where she wants to be. She has performed a perfect set, using the correct volume for her chest muscle group. She can rest assured that she has worked as many muscle fibers in her chest as possible and that her anaerobic system has done all the work. After a few days of rest and recovery, Jane might need to add 5 pounds to the bar for a total of 140 lbs to hit muscle failure within the 45 to 60 second time frame.

As your body adapts and strengthens, you will need to increase the lifting weight for each of your muscle groups over time to keep the volume of each set within the 45 to 60 second time range.

While performing an exercise, if you go beyond 60 seconds and you are nowhere near muscular failure, keep going until you hit failure. Next time you workout, correct the volume by adding 20% more weight to the bar. By using this method and keeping accurate records, you will see a steady and consistent increase in strength. You will also see visual results quickly in your muscle tone and fat loss.

Most people don't understand this concept. They visit the gym and lift moderate amounts of weight for an undetermined amount of reps and sets. Without high intensity levels, only slow and mid twitch muscle fibers are taxed. Slow and mid twitch muscle fibers don't grow quickly like fast twitch fibers, so results from this inferior lifting style are disappointing at best.

The most efficient strength training method is to perform the minimum amount of exercise (sets, reps, and rest between sets) with the maximum amount of intensity you can safely attain. This means going all out in the gym and putting everything you have into those 45 to 60 seconds without reserving even a fraction of your energy.

PROPER WARM-UP AND COOL-DOWN

Warming up before and cooling down after a workout are important parts of any strength training routine. Each workout should begin with a 5 to 10 minute warm-up on an aerobic exercise machine like a stationary bike or a treadmill. A brief aerobic warm-up gets the blood pumping and primes the muscular system to prepare for the intense anaerobic workout ahead.

A warm-up is not a workout in and of itself. An aerobic warm-up should be low in intensity—a good brisk walk rather than a flat-out sprint. After warming up, you should feel warm, but not fatigued; you should feel ready to workout, not finished. It is a mistake to turn an aerobic warm-up into a 20-minute full aerobic training session.

Two warm-up sets should be performed before each weight lifting exercise. The first should be 3 to 4 reps with 50% of the weight to be used in the working set. The second warm-up set should be 3 to 4 reps with 65% of the weight to be used in the working set. Warm-up sets are meant to prime the muscles and get the blood pumping, not to hit muscle failure. If, after 2 warm-up sets, you still feel cold, you may perform a third set at 65% of the working weight. Warm-up sets should feel easy and shouldn't burn much energy. Save the big guns for the actual working set.

A proper cool-down consists of a brief stretching routine for all muscle groups worked. The cool-down should also include a 5-minute low intensity walk on a treadmill, stationary bike or aerobic machine of your choice.

Warming up and cooling down are excellent ways to make sure your body performs at top efficiency during a weight-training workout. Warm-ups and cool-downs aid in the prevention of muscular injuries during workouts. They also help the body recover smoothly during rest and recovery time between workouts, lessening stiffness and soreness. No workout is complete without a proper warm-up and cool-down.

THE POWER OF LIFTING TECHNIQUE

Visit any gym and you will see that most people who workout don't know what they are doing. They rack up a set of free weights or an exercise machine and start throwing the weight around with no reason or purpose. They sit down and fire off 10 reps of dumbbell overhead presses in rapid succession. Within 20 seconds they have finished their set and are toweling beads of sweat from their foreheads. This couldn't be more wrong. Haphazardly throwing weight around without any thought of form or cadence is the best way to get hurt during a workout.

If safety is a priority, and it is, then cadence and form are important considerations. Along with offering safety, good cadence and form also guarantee that each muscle group is worked as effectively as possible.

Proper cadence and form requires purposeful movement. Purposeful movement is slow, controlled motion while performing an exercise. With purposeful movement, muscles work at maximum efficiency.

Inexperienced weight lifters often try to make exercises easier by throwing the weight past the most difficult parts of the movement. While doing a bench press, a beginner might push the weight rapidly up from his chest into a fully extended position. The rapid motion makes the exercise easier. After holding the weight in a fully extended position for a few seconds, the beginner might quickly drop the weight back to his chest, having the false idea that the bench press is the act of pressing the weight up, not lowering it back down. This method robs the exercise of its effectiveness and sets the lifter up for injury.

Quick, erratic movement, while lifting weights, is called *explosive lifting*. This type of lifting is unsafe. Explosive lifting exposes the body to dangerous acceleration, velocity, and momentum spikes. These spikes can cause loss of control over the weight and painful, possibly permanent, injuries.

Impact force occurs when downward momentum and upward momentum collide without a safety pause between. During a bench press, if the weight is dropped to the chest from a full, arm-extended position and pushed back up without a pause, there is incredible impact force. This high impact force can sometimes reach several times the actual weight being moved. A hundred pounds on a barbell can turn into several hundred pounds at the moment of impact due to momentum and deceleration forces; that's a dangerous amount of force.

Force of that magnitude can cause serious injuries like torn muscles, tendon strains, sprains and ligament injuries. Muscle connective tissue can even detach from bones and joints--OUCH!

47

The goal of effective weight training is to fire as much muscle fiber as possible. This can only be accomplished by using slow, purposeful movement while lifting weight. Throwing the weight works the muscles very little and hammers the joints.

Proper lifting cadence involves moving the weight slowly and evenly with the purpose of contracting as many muscle fibers as possible along the full length of the muscle. Purposeful movement exhausts muscle fibers thoroughly and limits strain on the joints.

Without purposeful movement, the whole idea of high intensity training is nullified. By throwing the weight, the maximum amount of muscular fiber will not be stimulated. You might get a few more reps into your set, but the whole set will be much less effective than if executed with slow, steady and controlled movement. Muscle contraction is the reason you lift weights; muscle contraction occurs best at slow lifting speeds.

Each exercise has its own cadence. Exercise cadence is based on the following three parts of the lifting sequence:

1. Move the weight from the beginning position to the ending position of the exercise.
2. Hold the weight in a full, contracted muscular position at the end of the exercise or in some compound exercises at the bottom stretched position.
3. Move the weight back to the beginning position of the exercise.

The proper cadence for a bench press is 5:2:5 (Figure 9-1). The bench press starts with the arms fully extended, the barbell in your hands at the top of the exercise. It should take a full 5 seconds to bring the weight down to a 90-degree position (both elbows bent to 90 degrees). There is a 2-second pause at the bottom of the movement to protect against impact forces to the pectoralis, triceps, and deltoids. After a 2-second pause, the weight is pushed back up to the top of the movement over a full 5-second count. This process is repeated until muscle failure is reached. It doesn't matter where muscle failure occurs. It can happen half way through the exercise or after a complete rep. What matters is that muscle failure is reached.

| BARBELL BENCH PRESS - CHEST | | CADENCE - 5:2:5 |

1 Using a loaded barbell, begin this exercise at the top of the movement with the arms just short of lock-out. Concentrating on the muscles of the chest, lower the barbell over a full 5-second count until your elbows are at 90-degree angles.

2 Hold in the bottom position with the elbows at 90-degree angles for a full 2-second count.

3 Concentrating on the muscles of the chest, move to the starting position of the exercise over a full 5-second count.

Figure 9-1

You will find in the appendix of this book a step-by-step guide that diagrams how to perform exercises for every major muscle group. Review these tutorials and use them as part of your workout routine.

NOTE:

Total Human has produced a valuable DVD that teaches the 89 most effective exercises. The DVD is packed with helpful videos that will teach you the proper way to perform each exercise. Each video illustrates primary and helper muscles worked. Shane teaches you the proper cadence for each exercise, detailing how to perform them using purposeful movement. Each exercise is hand selected for its ability to isolate certain muscles and work them as efficiently as possible.

This DVD and other excellent Total Human products are available at www.totalhuman.com.

WHICH EXERCISE WHEN?

For every muscle group to be worked as intensely as possible, exercises must be performed in the proper order. Workout sheets can be found in the appendix of this book that illustrate the best order in which to perform exercises.

It is best to start an exercise routine by training the largest muscle groups first and work down to the smallest groups. The muscles of the abdomen should be trained last. The reason for this involves 2 concepts: energy expenditure and stabilization.

ENERGY EXPENDITURE

There are two types of exercises, single joint exercises and compound exercises.

Single joint exercises involve the bending of only one joint and usually work one muscle group in isolation. An example of a single joint exercise is the barbell curl. The barbell curl involves only the bending of the elbow and works the bicep muscles in isolation.

Compound exercises involve the bending of 2 or more joints, working a primary muscle group, but enlisting the use of helper muscles. An example of a compound exercise is the bench press. The bench press involves the bending of the elbow and shoulder joints. The chest muscles are the primary muscles worked, but the deltoids and triceps also take part as helper muscles.

The difference between simple and compound exercises is an important consideration when determining exercise order. The bench press is primarily a chest exercise. The chest muscles are hearty and strong; but the deltoids and triceps also participate as helper muscles when performing the bench press. Being smaller and not having the force of the chest muscles, the deltoids and triceps usually become the limiting factor in performing the bench press. If the deltoid or tricep muscles are worked before performing the bench press, the ability to perform the bench press will be heavily impaired. The energy of the helper muscles will have been expended and won't be able to perform at their highest level and the chest won't be fully worked.

A better option is to perform the bench press to failure and save tricep and deltoid exercises for later in the routine. It is more efficient to train large muscle groups before training smaller, helper muscles.

STABILIZATION

The muscles of the abdomen and lower back (Figure 9-2) should be trained last. This is because of their important role in sustaining lumbar and pelvic stabilization during exercises that work the upper and lower body. Performing squats, bent rows, military press, or even pull downs can cause injuries to the lower back if the abdominal, obliques and erector spinae muscles of the waist and lower back are tired and can't contract at full force. In most cases it is not a good idea to perform abdominal and lower back exercises before compound exercises for the back, shoulders, or legs.

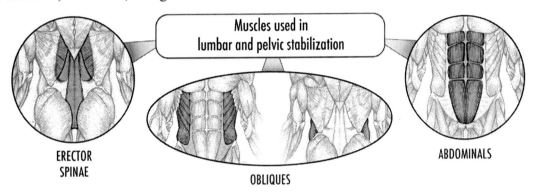

Muscles used in lumbar and pelvic stabilization

ERECTOR SPINAE

OBLIQUES

ABDOMINALS

Figure 9-2

Deadlifts (Figure 9-3) are an exception to this rule because they are the king of compound movements. Deadlifts are thought of as a lower back exercise, but they also train all muscles along the back of the body, with emphasis on the lower back, upper back, hamstrings, and trapezius muscles of the shoulder girdle and mid-back. They also work the quadriceps on the front part of the legs, the calves, the deltoids, the arms, and the abdominals.

BARBELL DEADLIFT - LOWER BACK | **CADENCE - 5:2:5**

1. Concentrating on the muscles in the lower back, descend to the bottom position in a full 5-second count. Make sure to keep the chest high and the back straight.

2. Remain in the bottom position for a 2-second count.

3. Concentrating on the muscles in your lower back, move to the starting position over a 5-second count.

Figure 9-3

Because deadlifts stress so many muscle groups and demand so much of the body, they should always be the first exercise performed in any routine. Since they work the muscles of the lower back they should not be done in any exercise session that also includes free weight squats (Figure 9-4) where the muscles of the lower back are needed for stabilization of the spine.

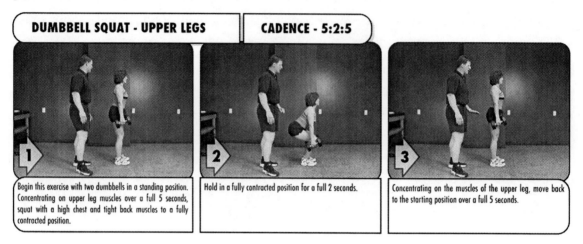

DUMBBELL SQUAT - UPPER LEGS | **CADENCE - 5:2:5**

1. Begin this exercise with two dumbbells in a standing position. Concentrating on upper leg muscles over a full 5 seconds, squat with a high chest and tight back muscles to a fully contracted position.

2. Hold in a fully contracted position for a full 2 seconds.

3. Concentrating on the muscles of the upper leg, move back to the starting position over a full 5 seconds.

Figure 9-4

FLEXIBILITY

Flexibility training is a valuable part of any workout; but heavy stretching at the beginning of a routine loosens tendons and muscles around the joints and decreases stability during weight or aerobic training. Strength training stresses not only the working muscles but also the tendons, ligaments, and joints. Weight training after loosening muscles, tendons, ligaments and joints with rigorous stretching can increase the chance of injury. A light stretch before strength training is a good idea, but a full flexibility training session should be saved until after aerobic or weight training.

After working out it is only necessary to stretch muscle groups that have been worked during the routine. This will help lessen soreness during rest and recovery time.

NOTE:

Tutorials outlining stretching exercises for all muscle groups can be found in the appendix of this book.

REST AND RECOVERY

It is vital to rest between high intensity workouts until all controlled muscular damage is repaired. It takes the body anywhere from 2 days to a full week or more to adequately repair muscle tissue and return to full strength.

Using a standard and hard-set resting period is a mistake. Many exercise programs advise resting for 48-hours between workouts. This is a dangerous practice. Working out without full recovery increases the chance of injury.

Resting periods should be calculated by reading your body's natural language. A beginner might only need 1 to 2 days rest between workouts. But, over time, with consistent workouts, muscle mass will build. Increased muscle mass means increased inroading of muscles during workouts. The more muscle mass gained, the longer it takes to fully recover between workouts. It is not unheard of for large body builders to require a full week or more between workouts to fully recover.

FITNESS MYTHS AND FALLACIES

The health and fitness industry has grown steadily over the past 3 decades into a multi-billion dollar business. There are hundreds of fitness plans out there. With so much information, it's easy to become confused. One week the fitness trends say one thing and another week the message changes. Some fitness plans even contradict each another.

When evaluating any fitness plan, the following question should be asked: is the plan truly based on the science of human physiology or is it merely the contrived opinion of someone who has never studied the human body in detail?

By understanding a few common fallacies, many fitness plans can be dispelled as hype and less-effective methods of training.

Let's take a look at some of these fallacies.

ONE SIZE FITS ALL

Your body is unique; it adapts and develops differently than anyone else's. The makeup of your muscular fiber distribution is individual. Your arms, legs and torso length are singular to you and have much to do with determining the best exercise for you.

If a workout program prescribes the same amount of exercises, reps and sets for everyone, beware; this type of program does not consider what makes you unique from other people. A standard workout sheet for the upper body using such a system might look like Figure 9-5.

MUSCLE GROUP	EXERCISE	SETS	REPS	WEIGHT
CHEST	BENCH PRESS	3	10	100 LBS.
SHOULDERS	MILITARY PRESS	3	10	60 LBS.
BICEPS	BARBELL CURLS	3	10	60 LBS.
TRICEPS	TRICEP EXTENSIONS	3	10	110 LBS.
ABDOMINALS	WEIGHTED CRUNCHES	3	10	25 LBS.
OBLIQUES	DUMBBELL SIDE BENDS	3	10	35 LBS.

Figure 9-5

This is a classic example of a one-size-fits-all workout plan.

Let's tear it apart.

First, this plan lacks one of the three basic measurements of volume; *time under load.* 3 sets of 10 bench presses means nothing to the muscles of your chest. How long should each bench press take? There is a huge difference between a 3 second bench press and a 10 second bench press.

Second, how is the amount of prescribed reps figured? Are 3 sets of 10 barbell curls right for everyone, including you, your friend Bill and the girl running on the treadmill on the other side of the gym? Remember, what works for others may not work for you.

Third, how is lifting weight figured? Is it just an arbitrary number thrown in for good measure? How will you know when it's time to increase or decrease the weight? Do you simply increase weight as you can handle it?

By following the HIT system, volume is measured by listening to your muscle system's natural feedback and determining the exact amount of volume needed for each muscle group.

HIT training allows you to learn the language of your body. You become the expert on you. Once you become adept at understanding what your body has to say, you don't need the objectivity of a qualified personal trainer. You become your own personal trainer. You will be able to tailor your workout plan for your body. Your workout plan will work better for you than for any other individual. Remember there is no such thing as one-size-fits-all when it comes to working out.

Bogus Exercises

There is a growing trend in the fitness arena to find new and different ways to exercise. Some exercise gurus prescribe weird exercises for obscure muscle groups in an effort to appear cutting edge. In most cases these obscure muscle groups act purely as helper muscles and should be worked accordingly.

While I am sure many a personal training client spends many a sleepless night agonizing into the wee hours of the morning over the state of his multifidus, transverse abdominils, or quadratus lumborum, the truth is these and most other buzzword muscles are trained through basic compound or single joint exercises.

Go to the appendix of this book for a list of excellent exercises. You will find instructions and diagrams that detail how to perform exercises for every muscle group.

Gimmicks

Watered down versions of physical therapy, wobble boards and rubber bands don't work well in a productive exercise program--especially as part of a strength training regimen. Resistance created by gimmicks like these is usually untrackable. It's impossible to know how much force is produced by a blue rubber band as opposed to a red rubber band. How do you know you're making progress if you can't track resistance?

A classic example of ineffective workout gimmicks is the wobble board. A wobble board is a piece of wood or hard plastic with an inflatable or hard plastic center that you stand on. The idea is if you can stand on the wobble board while performing exercise, you will increase strength and stability in your hips, lower back and work your abdominal muscles. Gimmicks like the wobble board are based on flimsy, flawed, or worse, no research. They are designed to take your money and put another useless gimmick into your closet.

The body is developed by stress and adaptation; the greater the stress, the greater the adaptation. If you work or stress your muscles beyond the threshold of normal operation and give them adequate rest between workouts, they will adapt to a higher level of performance to better handle the higher level of stress. If stress is below that threshold there will be NO adaptation. Your body will not commit the needed resources to improve unless it is required.

The perceived improvement gained by training with a gimmick like the wobble board is nothing but neuromuscular adaptation, or motor learning skills. These neuromuscular patterns will only help you balance better on the wobble board. The skills you gain will not translate to other muscular tasks such as standing on a stable floor.

If your goal is to become really good at standing on a wobbling 12 inch piece of wood, then by all means, stand on a wobble board. But if your goal is more stable ankles, knees and hips, focus on strengthening the muscles surrounding those specific joints in a safe, trackable way with measurable resistance and proper exercise technique.

An argument for gimmicks is that you need variation in your routine so you don't get bored. It's good to mix up your routine so it doesn't get old, but the truth is productive training is hard work. If you make the mental and physical commitment to a goal of seeing hard-line results then, with the help of this book, you can have the body you want.

REPS

There are many theories about exactly how many reps should be performed in each set. A common theory is that you should perform 3 to 5 reps per set to build strength, 6 to 10 reps to start your body into the growth process and 12 to 15 reps for muscular endurance. This theory can be dispelled with a few logical questions. What happens after 15 reps? Since I am not building strength, size, or endurance, what am I training for? What if I perform 5 1/2 reps, will I build strength and size? Can I really build strength without size or size without strength? Does cadence have anything to do with it? What if I lift 5 reps with a slow cadence and an additional 2 with a fast cadence, does the rep range still apply?

The truth is it doesn't matter how many reps are in a set, as long as each rep is performed with proper form and cadence and the muscles run out of steam between 45 and 60 seconds.

SETS

Inferior exercise programs often assign an arbitrary amount of sets as part of an exercise routine (i.e., 3 sets of 10 bench presses every 3 days). Each person is unique. It is impossible to assign the same amount of sets to every individual and expect everyone to have the same results.

The truth is, in most cases, a single set of exercise to muscle failure is all that is needed to stimulate muscles into the growth process. Extra sets are, for the most part, of no value.

Time Under Load to muscle failure is the most efficient way to analyze the effectiveness of a set. It is less effective to analyze a set's efficiency based on how many reps of an exercise are performed during a set or even worse, to limit one's self to a set number of reps per set.

SHAPING EXERCISES

Another in-the-gym falsehood is that performing multiple exercises at different angles can work different parts of the same muscle to bring out more quality and shape.

Some believe that the decline bench press brings out the lower pec, the incline bench press brings out the upper pec and the flat bench press bring out the mid pec. This is false. The muscles of the chest have a common origin; they are connected to the skeleton by the same tendons. When a nerve message is sent to cause muscle fibers in the chest to contract, all muscle fibers attached to that nerve fire and contract; not some, but all. It's impossible to isolate certain portions of the chest muscles and exclude others. Muscle fibers contract in an all or none fashion, meaning they either contract fully or not at all. Exercise angle and range has little or nothing to do with which fibers contract. The only real factor is the amount of resistance muscle fibers must contract against.

You are genetically built with certain muscle lengths and shapes. The idea that you can train for shape can be shot down with common sense. Pick a shape, an oblong, or a hexagon and try to train your bicep muscles to take on that shape. It can't be done. But it doesn't stop some from prescribing exercises to bring out the peak of the biceps, or to add shape to particular muscles.

Characteristics of muscle shape and size are genetic and can't be changed. Some people are flexible and well proportioned; others are blocky and thick. Some, regardless of which training program they use, never gain much muscle mass at all.

Another problem with peaking and shaping exercises is that they are usually performed with minimal weight and are in the body's weakest biomechanical positions. By using these awkward exercises, the amount of muscle fibers worked is limited. The whole idea goes against muscle growth stimulation. For best results, the maximum amount of muscle fibers must be worked in an optimal time period (45 to 60 seconds).

CHAPTER SUMMARY

PRINCIPLES

WEIGHT TRAINING

- The 4 components of weight training are: volume, intensity, duration and frequency.
  - o Volume is the amount of work the muscles do.
  - o Intensity is the level of exhaustion muscles reach during a unit of time working out.
  - o Duration is the total amount of time spent in one workout including rest times between sets of exercise.
  - o Frequency is how often workouts are performed.
- Intensity should dictate volume.
  - o The goal is to hit muscle failure between 45 and 60 seconds of exercise.
- A proper warm-up and cool-down are essential to any workout.
- Warm-up sets with reduced weight should be done for each exercise before lifting the working weight.
- Purposeful motion means slow, even movement during exercise to increase intensity and decrease the chance of injury.
- Except in specialized routines, exercises should be ordered to work larger muscle groups first and work down to the smallest muscle groups last.
- Heavy stretching prior to weight training can loosen joints and cause injury during intense weight lifting.
- It is necessary to rest between workouts until all muscles are fully recovered.
- Avoid one-size-fits-all workout plans.
- Most exercise gimmicks are useless.
- Reps are irrelevant; cadence must dictate the number of reps in a set. If muscle failure is reached between 45 and 60 seconds while using slow, controlled movement, then the correct number of reps has been performed.
- One set to muscular failure is usually all that is needed to force muscles into the growth and adaptation process.
- Specific muscles can't be shaped. Traits of size and proportion are genetic

CHAPTER 10: ANAEROBIC CONDITIONING: A STEP-BY-STEP PLAN

APPLICATION

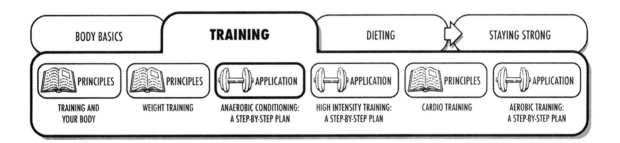

CHAPTER PREVIEW

Newcomers to strength training should condition their bodies before diving into high intensity training. Conditioning doesn't involve lifting weight to muscle failure. Conditioning is a time to ease the body into weightlifting regimen and limit muscle soreness. Conditioning workouts are a time to get familiar with proper cadence and form.

CONDITIONING FOR HIGH INTENSITY TRAINING

If you are a newcomer to weight training or if you haven't worked out for a while, it is highly recommended that you condition your body before diving headlong into a HIT training regimen. If you visit the gym regularly, you can probably skip this step.

Conditioning before starting a HIT regimen will help your body transition from a sedentary life-style to high intensity training as smoothly as possible. Kicking in a full high intensity training program can shock your body if you are not prepared, causing pain and muscular dysfunction for the first couple of weeks of heavy training.

Conditioning will help your body become acquainted with lifting weight as a form of anaerobic exercise. It is an opportunity to learn to use slow, controlled cadence with every exercise.

Make a few copies of the conditioning worksheet, provided in the appendix of this book, and take them to the gym with you to record what happens during your conditioning workouts.

The conditioning worksheet introduces you to 6 exercises. These 6 exercises are meant to help you learn proper form and cadence and work your entire body while you are at it.

The 6 exercises are:

- Barbell Squat (Figure 10-1)
- Barbell Compound Row (Figure 10-2)
- Barbell Deadlift (Figure 10-3)
- Barbell Bench Press (Figure 10-4)
- Barbell Overhead Press (Figure 10-5)
- Barbell Preacher Curl (Figure 10-6)

Review the proper cadence and form of each exercise used on the conditioning worksheet before visiting the gym. Below are tutorials on how to perform the 6 conditioning exercises.

BARBELL SQUAT - UPPER LEGS | CADENCE - 5:2:5

Begin this exercise with a loaded barbell held over the shoulders in a standing position. Concentrating on the upper leg muscles, squat with a high chest and tight back muscles over a full 5-second count to the bottom position.

Hold in the bottom position for a full 2-second count.

Concentrating on the muscles of the upper legs, move back to the starting position over a full 5-second count.

Figure 10-1

BARBELL COMPOUND ROW - UPPER BACK | CADENCE - 6:2:6

Begin this exercise with a loaded barbell in deadlift position with a high chest and tight back. Concentrating on the upper back muscles, lift the barbell over a 6-second count to a contracted position.

Hold in a fully contracted position with the elbows bent to 90-degree angles for a full 2-second count.

Concentrating on the muscles in the upper back, lower the barbell back to starting position over a full 6-second count.

Figure 10-2

BARBELL DEADLIFT - LOWER BACK | CADENCE - 5:2:5

Concentrating on the muscles in the lower back, descend to the bottom position in a full 5-second count. Make sure to keep the chest high and the back straight.

Remain in the bottom position for a 2-second count.

Concentrating on the muscles in your lower back, move to the starting position over a 5-second count.

Figure 10-3

BARBELL BENCH PRESS - CHEST | **CADENCE - 5:2:5**

Using a loaded barbell, begin this exercise at the top of the movement with the arms just short of lock-out. Concentrating on the muscles of the chest, lower the barbell over a full 5-second count until your elbows are at 90-degree angles.

Hold in the bottom position with the elbows at 90-degree angles for a full 2-second count.

Concentrating on the muscles of the chest, move to the starting position of the exercise over a full 5-second count.

Figure 10-4

NOTE:

Other exercise tutorials, teaching correct technique, form and cadence, can be found in the appendix of this book.

Take a copy of the conditioning worksheet--(Figure 10-4) found in APPENDIX E: CONDITIONING WORKSHEET--to the gym or to your home gym. Following is an example of the conditioning worksheet. Remember that conditioning workouts should be performed with less weight and less volume in order to ready your body for full High Intensity Training.

CONDITIONING WORKSHEET

1. WARM-UP

ACTIVITY	TIME

2. EXERCISES

MUSCLE GROUP	EXERCISE	WEIGHT	REPS	TUL	EVALUATION QUESTIONS
UPPER LEGS	Barbell Squat Cadence (5:2:5) Total Time 12 sec				Are you comfortable with the exercise form? YES◯ NO◯ Are you comfortable with the exercise cadence? YES◯ NO◯ Are you comfortable performing the exercise? YES◯ NO◯ How was the weight? TOO LIGHT◯ JUST RIGHT◯ TOO HEAVY◯ How do you feel after finishing the exercise? NOT FATIGUED◯ MEDIUM FATIGUE◯ FATIGUED◯ HEAVY FATIGUE◯
UPPER BACK	Barbell Compound Row Cadence (6:2:6) Total Time 14 sec				Are you comfortable with the exercise form? YES◯ NO◯ Are you comfortable with the exercise cadence? YES◯ NO◯ Are you comfortable performing the exercise? YES◯ NO◯ How was the weight? TOO LIGHT◯ JUST RIGHT◯ TOO HEAVY◯ How do you feel after finishing the exercise? NOT FATIGUED◯ MEDIUM FATIGUE◯ FATIGUED◯ HEAVY FATIGUE◯
LOWER BACK	Barbell Deadlift Cadence (5:2:5) Total Time 12 sec				Are you comfortable with the exercise form? YES◯ NO◯ Are you comfortable with the exercise cadence? YES◯ NO◯ Are you comfortable performing the exercise? YES◯ NO◯ How was the weight? TOO LIGHT◯ JUST RIGHT◯ TOO HEAVY◯ How do you feel after finishing the exercise? NOT FATIGUED◯ MEDIUM FATIGUE◯ FATIGUED◯ HEAVY FATIGUE◯
CHEST	Barbell Bench Press Cadence (5:2:5) Total Time 12 sec				Are you comfortable with the exercise form? YES◯ NO◯ Are you comfortable with the exercise cadence? YES◯ NO◯ Are you comfortable performing the exercise? YES◯ NO◯ How was the weight? TOO LIGHT◯ JUST RIGHT◯ TOO HEAVY◯ How do you feel after finishing the exercise? NOT FATIGUED◯ MEDIUM FATIGUE◯ FATIGUED◯ HEAVY FATIGUE◯
SHOULDERS	Barbell Overhead Press Cadence (5:2:5) Total Time 12 sec				Are you comfortable with the exercise form? YES◯ NO◯ Are you comfortable with the exercise cadence? YES◯ NO◯ Are you comfortable performing the exercise? YES◯ NO◯ How was the weight? TOO LIGHT◯ JUST RIGHT◯ TOO HEAVY◯ How do you feel after finishing the exercise? NOT FATIGUED◯ MEDIUM FATIGUE◯ FATIGUED◯ HEAVY FATIGUE◯
BICEPS	Barbell Preacher Curl Cadence (5:2:5) Total Time 14 sec				Are you comfortable with the exercise form? YES◯ NO◯ Are you comfortable with the exercise cadence? YES◯ NO◯ Are you comfortable performing the exercise? YES◯ NO◯ How was the weight? TOO LIGHT◯ JUST RIGHT◯ TOO HEAVY◯ How do you feel after finishing the exercise? NOT FATIGUED◯ MEDIUM FATIGUE◯ FATIGUED◯ HEAVY FATIGUE◯

3. COOL-DOWN

ACTIVITY	TIME

4. FLEXIBILITY

MUSCLE GROUP	COMPLETED STRETCH
UPPER LEGS	YES◯ NO◯
UPPER BACK	YES◯ NO◯
LOWER BACK	YES◯ NO◯
CHEST	YES◯ NO◯
SHOULDERS	YES◯ NO◯
BICEPS	YES◯ NO◯

5. EVALUATION

POST-WORKOUT PERSONAL EVALUATION
Are you comfortable with the exercise form? YES◯ NO◯
Are you comfortable with the exercise cadence? YES◯ NO◯
Are you comfortable performing exercises? YES◯ NO◯
How do you feel after the workout? NOT FATIGUED◯ MEDIUM FATIGUE◯ FATIGUED◯ HEAVY FATIGUE◯

Figure 10-5

The sheet is divided into the following 4 sections:

1. Warm-up
2. Exercise
3. Cool-down
4. Stretching
5. Evaluate the routine

CONDITIONING STEP 1: WARM-UP

The first item on the conditioning worksheet is *warm-up*. To warm-up, pick a cardiovascular workout machine of your choice; some good options are a treadmill, elliptical or stationary bike. You can also hit the road for a jog. Warming-up gets the blood pumping and the muscles primed. A warm-up should not be a full aerobic workout. 5 to 10 minutes at an easy pace is sufficient. After warming-up, write which aerobic exercise you chose and how many minutes you performed the exercise in the provided boxes on your conditioning sheet (Figure 10-5).

Figure 10-6

CONDITIONING STEP 2: EXERCISE

Now that your muscles are ready to be worked, it's time to perform the 6 conditioning exercises on the conditioning worksheet. Performing conditioning exercises consists of the following 3 steps:

1. Pick a weight
2. Do the exercise
3. Answer the evaluation questions

PICK A WEIGHT

Before performing each exercise, pick a lifting weight that is comfortable for you--not too heavy and not too light. You don't want a weight that you can perform a hundred reps with or one that will burn you out in the first rep. During the conditioning phase, the idea is not to exhaust your muscles; your goal is to get familiar with correct lifting form and cadence. Write the lifting weight into the appropriate box for each exercise (Figure 10-9).

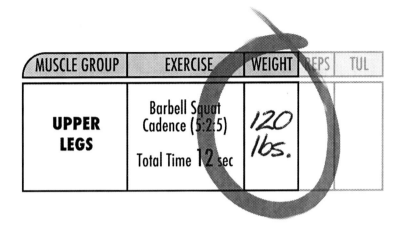

MUSCLE GROUP	EXERCISE	WEIGHT	REPS	TUL
UPPER LEGS	Barbell Squat Cadence (5:2:5) Total Time 12 sec	120 lbs.		

Figure 10-7

DO THE EXERCISE

You need a stopwatch for this step. Following is a timeline detailing how to properly perform one set of a conditioning routine exercise.

1. Start the clock.
2. Perform a short set of the exercise. Just do a few reps, maybe 3 or 4--keep it light. Again, you are not out to hit muscle failure at this point. Your goal is to get familiar with the proper cadence and form of each exercise and get an idea of what weight is right for you for each exercise.
3. Stop the clock at the end of the set. The total time it takes you to perform the set is your time under load (TUL).
4. Log the reps and TUL for the set. After each exercise, write the quantity of reps and the time under load (TUL) in the provided boxes on the conditioning worksheet. You can evaluate your cadence by dividing the number of seconds by the number of reps and comparing the calculation with the total time for the exercise. Using the conditioning form as illustrated in Figure 10-7, if you divide 36 (the TUL) by 3 (the number of reps), you get 12 seconds. 12 seconds is the total time it should take to complete 1 barbell squat (5:2:5 cadence = 5+2+5=12 seconds)--a perfect cadence.

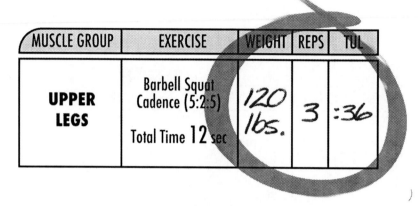

Figure 10-8

ANSWER THE EVALUATION QUESTIONS

On the conditioning worksheet, each exercise has its own 5-question mini-questionnaire. Answer these questions directly after finishing each exercise. This will help you get a feel for each exercise and an understanding of cadence and form.

Your goal is to pick a weight and perform each exercise with proper cadence and be able to honestly fill out the exercise questionnaire on the conditioning as shown in Figure 10-8.

EVALUATION QUESTIONS			
Are you comfortable with the exercise form?	YES ⊗ NO ◯		
Are you comfortable with the exercise cadence?	YES ⊗ NO ◯		
Are you comfortable performing the exercise?	YES ⊗ NO ◯		
How was the weight?	TOO LIGHT ◯	JUST RIGHT ⊗	TOO HEAVY ◯
How do you feel after finishing the exercise?	NOT FATIGUED ◯	MEDIUM FATIGUE ◯	FATIGUED ⊗ HEAVY FATIGUE ◯

Figure 10-9

CONDITIONING STEP 3: COOL DOWN

After finishing all 6 exercises, it's time to cool-down. Jump on the aerobic machine of your choice; the stationary bike and treadmill are good options. Exercise at a comfortable pace for 5 to 10 minutes. This will help relieve stress and soreness in the muscles after your workout.

CONDITIONING STEP 4: STRETCHING

You can further decrease stress and soreness by stretching after each workout. Stretching exercises for all 6 muscle groups worked during conditioning workouts are illustrated in Figure 10-9 and Figure 10-10.

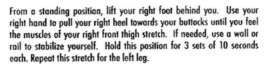

STRETCHES

Calf Stretch
Muscles stretched: Calves

Use a wall to stabilize yourself. Standing in a split legged position with your left foot back and your right foot forward, apply pressure to your left foot until you feel the muscles of your left calf stretch. Hold this position for 3 sets of 10 seconds each. Repeat this stretch for the right leg.

Front Thigh Stretch
Muscles stretched: Quadriceps

From a standing position, lift your right foot behind you. Use your right hand to pull your right heel towards your buttocks until you feel the muscles of your right front thigh stretch. If needed, use a wall or rail to stabilize yourself. Hold this position for 3 sets of 10 seconds each. Repeat this stretch for the left leg.

Hamstring and Lower Back Stretch
Muscles stretched: Hamstrings and Erector Spinae

Place your right heel on a stable platform like a rail or table. Lock the knee and lean forward, bending your lower back until you feel the muscles of your right hamstring and lower back stretch. Hold this position for 3 sets of 10 seconds each. Repeat this stretch for the left leg.

Outer Thigh and Glute Stretch
Muscles stretched: Outer Thigh and Glutes

From a sitting position, bend the right knee and place your right foot on the outside of your left knee in a cross-legged position. Using your right hand, push your right knee across your body until you feel the muscles of your right glute and thigh stretch. Hold this position for 3 sets of 10 seconds each. Repeat this stretch for the left leg.

Front Thigh Stretch
Muscles Stretched: Quadriceps

Step forward with your left foot into a lunge position. Lower your body until you are over your bent left knee and your palms are against the floor. Rock your left foot back on the toe until you feel the muscles of your right hip and thigh stretch. Hold this position for 3 sets of 10 seconds each. Repeat this stretch for the left leg.

Figure 10-10

STRETCHES (CONTINUED)

Lower Back and Glute Stretch
Muscles stretched: Gluteus, Erector Spinea, and Hip Muscles

While lying on your back. Use your hands to draw your right knee to your chest until you feel the muscles of your lower back and glute stretch. Hold this position for 3 sets of 10 seconds each. Repeat this stretch for the other leg.

Lower Back, Obliques, and Outer Thigh Stretch
Erector Spinae, Obliques and Outer Thigh

While lying on your back, bend your right knee and place your right foot on the outside of your left knee in a cross-legged position. Using your left hand, pull the right knee across your body until you feel the muscles of your right oblique and outer thigh stretch. Hold this position for 3 sets of 10 seconds each.

Triceps and Lat Stretch
Muscles stretched: Triceps, Latissimus Dorsi and Obliques

While standing, bend your right elbow and hold it with your left hand. Use your left hand to draw your right elbow inward, behind your head until you feel the muscles of your triceps and lats stretch. Hold this position for 3 sets of 10 seconds each. Repeat this stretch with the left arm.

Broomstick Stretch
Muscles stretched: Anterior Deltoids, Biceps and Pectoral

From a standing position, hold a broomstick with an underhanded grip behind your back. Raise the broomstick behind your back until you feel the muscles of your pecs, anterior deltoids and biceps stretch. Hold this position for 3 sets of 10 seconds each.

Neck Stretch
Muscles stretched: Trapezius

While standing, tilt your head to the left, looking straight forward, until you feel the muscles of your right trapezius stretch. Hold this position for 3 sets of 10 seconds each. Repeat this exercise for the left trapezius.

Figure 10-11

It is only necessary to stretch the muscle groups worked during your workout. Remember to wait on heavy stretching until after you have performed all your exercises to make sure there is adequate support in the joints while lifting heavy weight.

CONDITIONING STEP 5: EVALUATE THE ROUTINE

The last step of an effective conditioning workout is to evaluate your entire routine after you have finished. There is a post workout mini-questionnaire on the conditioning work sheet for this purpose. This questionnaire helps you to evaluate your overall feel after performing an entire conditioning routine. Fill this questionnaire out after you finish working out, but before you leave the gym.

Your goal during conditioning is to answer the post-workout questions honestly on the conditioning work sheet as shown in Figure 10-11.

POST-WORKOUT PERSONAL EVALUATION		
Are you comfortable with the exercise form?	YES ⊗ NO ◯	
Are you comfortable with the exercise cadence?	YES ⊗ NO ◯	
Are you comfortable performing exercises?	YES ⊗ NO ◯	
How do you feel after the workout?	NOT FATIGUED ◯ MEDIUM FATIGUE ◯ FATIGUED ⊗ HEAVY FATIGUE ◯	

Figure 10-12

CONDITIONING STEP 6: ADD WEIGHT AND DO IT AGAIN

After a successful conditioning workout, wait for at least 2 days for your muscles to recover, increase the weight of each exercise by 5% and go back to the gym or your home gym for another conditioning workout. It will take 3 to 6 conditioning workouts before your body is ready for high-intensity training.

Much of conditioning has to do with how you feel. If you are sore and miserable after light conditioning workouts, continue conditioning until you feel healthy and ready to move on. High intensity training will work your muscles hard. Make sure that you are up to the challenge by using conditioning workouts to prepare your body. As soon as you feel ready, move on to the next phase; high intensity training.

CHAPTER SUMMARY

APPLICATION

CONDITIONING: A STEP-BY-STEP GUIDE

- Beginners should condition their bodies using the conditioning worksheet in the appendix of this book.
- Conditioning prepares the body for a full high intensity training regimen.
- Each conditioning routine should contain the following steps:
    - o Warm-up
    - o Exercise
    - o Cool Down
    - o Stretching
    - o Evaluate the routine as a whole
- Full rest and recovery should occur between workouts.
- The conditioning routine is meant as a means to get acquainted with exercise form and cadence.
- Muscle failure is not the goal during conditioning routines.
- Conditioning sets should only consist of 3 to 4 reps.

CHAPTER 11: HIGH INTENSITY TRAINING: A STEP-BY-STEP PLAN

APPLICATION

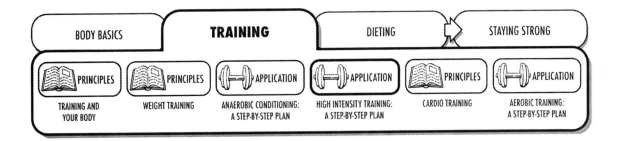

CHAPTER PREVIEW

High intensity training requires deep commitment to regular workouts and a willingness to go all out while lifting weights. All muscles groups can be worked in one workout or broken into 2 or 3 shorter workouts. Each workout consists of selecting routines, selecting working weights, warming up, performing exercise with warm-up sets, cooling down and stretching. Rest and recovery time is necessary between workouts to allow muscle growth.

STRENGTH TRAINING

Engaging in an effective strength-training regimen requires more than just visiting the gym 1 to 3 times a week and lifting weights. It takes mental focus, organization and an eye for detail. Part of your strength training practice should be thorough planning and record keeping. This book provides everything you need to prepare for workouts and to make sure that your workouts are executed with maximum efficiency.

This chapter is divided into two sections; preparation and working out. Both sections are sub-divided into their own step-by-step methods. With careful planning and effective workout habits, as outlined, you will see excellent strength gains, muscle tone improvement and fat loss.

PREPARATION STEP 1: COMMITMENT

You should now be conditioned and ready to go. You understand the principles of cadence and form. It's time to dive into a full-on high intensity training regimen. You must make the commitment to train with maximum intensity, giving your all to every set of exercise. Muscle failure is your goal. Gear up mentally for the work you will be doing in the gym. Commit to giving high intensity training every ounce of your energy and you will experience rapid and satisfying results.

PREPARATION STEP 2: SELECT ROUTINES AND EXERCISES

Three different workout sheet sets are located in the appendix of this book. You will find a full-body (Figure 11-1), all-in-one-day workout sheet, a 2-day break out sheet set and a 3-day break out sheet set. Each sheet represents 1 cycle of exercise for your entire body.

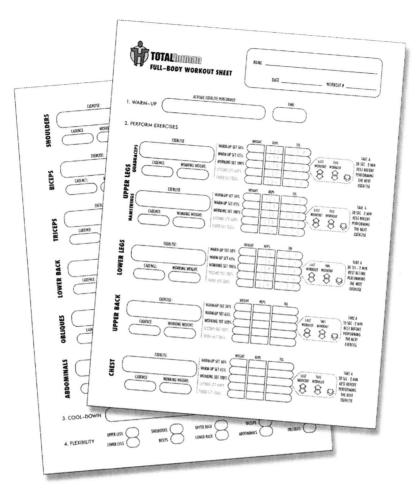

Figure 11-1

Each sheet set is designed to work all muscle groups effectively in either 1 workout session or broken up into 2 or 3 workout sessions. The order of exercises on each sheet works large muscle groups first and works down to smaller, helper muscle groups last.

The multiple workout sheet sets should be performed on different days. If you decide to use the 2-day workout sheet set, sheet 1 should be performed as an entire workout in 1 session. After rest and recovery days, sheet 2 should be performed as an entire workout in 1 session. This pattern should be cycled consistently; *sheet 1...rest and recovery...sheet 2...rest and recovery...sheet 1...rest and recovery...sheet 2....*

Before working out, select exercises you enjoy most from the exercise tutorials in the Appendix and write them on your workout sheet as in Figure 11-2. Write the cadence for each exercise in the provided box as well.

EXERCISE:

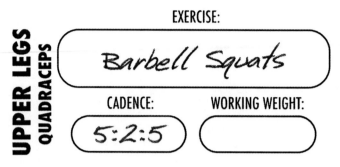

UPPER LEGS **QUADRACEPS**

Barbell Squats

CADENCE:

5:2:5

WORKING WEIGHT:

Figure 11-2

After selecting your favorite exercises, stick with them. Some trainers say that if you perform the same set of exercises every workout, without variation, your muscles will stop progressing; this is a myth. The truth is if you work a muscle correctly, even with the same repeated exercise, no matter how many times you perform that exercise you will experience additional muscle growth and toning.

Trackability is another benefit of sticking to a consistent set of exercises; it is easier to log the progress of each muscle group if you don't complicate your routine by choosing different exercises each time you workout.

As you finish each workout, bind all workout sheets into your success journal (the success journal is covered later in this book.); they are a valuable record of your progress. If you follow the concepts in this book, concrete, trackable results are guaranteed and seeing success is the greatest motivator.

PREPARATION STEP 3: SELECT WORKING WEIGHT

Select a working weight for each exercise that will cause muscular failure between 45 and 60 seconds. Remember that after 120 seconds of lifting, the aerobic energy system takes over and weight training for toning and shaping your body becomes next to useless. If the working weight you select does not cause you to hit muscle failure in 45 to 60 seconds, don't worry about it, you can adjust the working weight on your next workout. As you progress and your muscles strengthen you will need to add weight to each exercise to keep load times to muscular failure between 45 and 60 seconds. Write the working weight for each exercise in the provided boxes on your workout sheet (Figure 11-3).

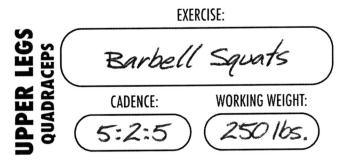

Figure 11-3

A good list of exercises can be found in Appendix B. Study the exercise tutorials. The tutorials have been categorized by muscle group. Cadence follows a number-colon-number-colon-number convention. The cadence for bicep curls is 6:2:6 (Figure 11-4).

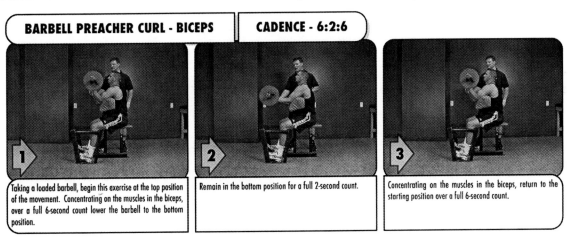

Figure 11-4

Before performing any exercise, use the exercise tutorials in the appendix to review form and cadence.

NOTE:
Total Human offers a DVD packed with step-by-step exercise video tutorials. The Total Human 88 Life-Changing Exercises DVD teaches how to perform 88 exercises especially selected by Shane Provstgaard. Each exercise is taught, one on one, by Shane himself. The DVD contains over an hour and a half of video. This DVD is offered at a reasonable price to help you get up to speed on the best exercises to lock in strength training success. For more information visit www.totalhuman.com.

WORKING OUT STEP 1: WARM-UP

It's time to go to the gym, or to your home-gym, and exercise. Take your workout sheet with you; it will act as a road map to get you through your entire routine.

Before performing any strength training exercises, make sure to warm-up by doing 5 to 10 minutes of low intensity exercise on an aerobic machine of your choice. Some good options are treadmill, elliptical or stationary bicycle. You can also hit the streets for a light jog.

Remember that this is not a time to engage in an exhaustive aerobic workout. Your warm-up goal is to get the blood pumping and prime the muscles for the high intensity workout ahead. After you have finished your warm-up, write the exercise you performed and how long you performed that exercise in the provided boxes on your workout sheet (Figure 11-5).

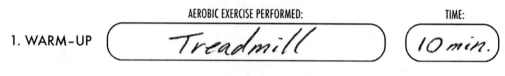

Figure 11-5

WORKING OUT STEP 2: PERFORM EXERCISES

Each exercise must be performed with slow, purposeful movement. Use the cadence you wrote on the workout sheet as a guide. There are three parts of exercise cadence: movement, hold and return movement. Perform each exercise with slow, purposeful movement; pause in a fully contracted position; then return the weight slowly and evenly in complete control to the starting position. With a slow, controlled lifting cadence, maximum muscle fibers will be worked.

Work your way down the workout sheet one muscle group at a time. There are 4 steps to each exercise:

1. Warm-up sets
2. Working set
3. 2-minute rest
4. Move to the next muscle group

WARM-UP SETS

Before performing a working set, perform 2 warm-up sets of exercise. The first warm-up set should consist of 3 to 6 reps of exercise with 50% of the total working weight. The second warm-up set should consist of 3 to 6 reps with 65% of the total working weight. Take a 2-minute break between the 2 warm-up sets.

If you have 30-pound dumbbell curls on your workout sheet for the bicep muscle group, your first warm-up set should consist of 3 to 4 reps with 15 pound dumbbells. Your second warm-up set should consist of 3 to 4 reps with 20-pound dumbbells.

Warm-up sets are meant to prime the muscles for high intensity lifting sets and to help hedge against injury. Warm-up sets should be light. Don't work to muscle failure on warm-up sets. The idea is to prep the muscles for heavy lifting, not to wear them out. These sets should feel easy and relaxed.

WORKING SETS

After performing warm-up sets, rack up the working weight, as you have written it on your workout sheet. It is vital that you track your time under load (TUL) during each set of exercise. To do this, start your stopwatch and perform the exercise with proper cadence until you hit muscle failure. Stop the clock directly after muscle failure and write the time on your workout sheet under TUL.

Figure 11-6

Figure 11-6 shows the muscle group as biceps; the exercise as dumbbell curls; the cadence as 6:2:6; the weight as 30 pounds. With 30-pound dumbbells, muscle failure was reached at 55 seconds during the first set of exercise.

One set of exercise to muscle failure is usually enough to inroad the muscles and start the muscle growth process, as long as failure occurs between 45 and 60 seconds. A second set of exercise may be useful if you can maintain a time under load to failure of 80% or more of the first set's time under load to failure.

A third set is rarely useful, but if you can maintain a time under load to failure of 80% or more of the time under load to failure of the first set, you may perform a third set. There is never a need to perform more than 3 sets of exercise for any muscle group. Always take a 30-second to 2-minute rest between sets. Your individual recovery will dictate the best rest time. Rest only as long as needed between sets. Don't sit around too long—-the clock is ticking.

MULTIPLE SETS OF EXERCISE			
EXERCISE	TIME UNDER LOAD	% OF FIRST SET TUL	IS THIS SET EFFECTIVE?
SET #1 - BENCH PRESS	55 SECONDS	N/A	N/A
• • • 2 MINUTE REST • • •			
SET #2 - BENCH PRESS	50 SECONDS	91%	YES, ABOVE 80%
• • • 2 MINUTE REST • • •			
SET #3 - BENCH PRESS	39 SECONDS	71%	NO, BELOW 80%

Figure 11-7

Figure 11-7 illustrates the use of multiple sets of exercise. You perform a set of bench presses and hit muscle failure at 55 seconds. You time a 2-minute rest. Using the same weight as in set #1, you perform a second set of bench presses and hit muscle failure at 50 seconds. 50 seconds is 91% of 55 seconds; the second set's time under load is above 80% of the first set's time under load to failure. You time another 2-minute rest and go for a third set. Again using the same weight as used in set #1, you perform the third set and hit muscle failure at 39 seconds. A quick calculation shows that 39 seconds is 71% of 55 seconds--not good enough. The third set's time under load to failure is not above 80% of the first set and will therefore be of no value.

The example in Figure 11-7 would be logged on a workout sheet as in Figure 11-8.

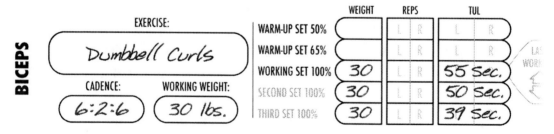

Figure 11-8

After determining that multiple sets are not helpful, there is no need to try to perform multiple sets again and again on every workout. The above diagram indicates that on subsequent workouts it is not necessary to perform a third set of dumbbell curls because the time under load to muscle failure is less than 80% of the time under load to muscle failure of the first set. Over time, as muscles grow and develop, the second set might be dropped as well.

2-minute Rest

After finishing 2 warm-up sets and 1 to 3 working sets for a muscle group, you must time a 30-second to 2-minute rest before moving onto the next muscle group. Every minute of your workout is important whether it be lifting time or resting time. Keep your workout moving along; stay engaged. You should be either lifting or timing 30-second to 2-minute breaks between sets. If you stop to socialize with others at the gym, you are diluting your workout and lowering the overall intensity. Stay focused, save the social life for after your workout.

Move to the Next Muscle Group

After a 30-second to 2-minute rest, move down the workout sheet to the next muscle group. Continue this process; warm-up sets, working set(s), 30-second to 2-minute rest. Move from muscle group to muscle group until you have worked through all muscle groups from top to bottom.

After you finish the *Workout* portion of your workout sheet, you are ready to move on to the next step; cool-down.

Working Out Step 3: Cool-down

A proper cool-down is an excellent way to tell your body that your workout is complete. A cool-down will relax the muscles and help relieve soreness between workouts.

After working out, choose an aerobic exercise of your choice. Some good options are treadmill, elliptical or stationary bike. A light road-jog is also a good choice. Perform 5 to 10 minutes of medium to low intensity aerobic exercise. Write the exercise you performed during your cool-down and the time you spent performing it on your workout sheet as in Figure 11-9.

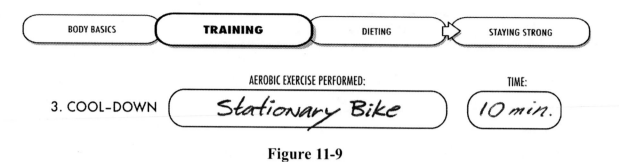

3. COOL-DOWN

AEROBIC EXERCISE PERFORMED: *Stationary Bike*   TIME: *10 min.*

Figure 11-9

WORKING OUT STEP 4: FLEXIBILITY

After your cool-down, stretch each muscle group worked during your workout. It is only necessary to stretch muscle groups included on your workout sheet. Tutorials on how to stretch each muscle group can be found in the appendix of this book. Stretching will help relieve soreness during the recovery process.

WORKING OUT STEP 5: REST AND RECOVERY

Full muscular recovery between workouts is one of the most important parts of the process. Lifting weights inroads muscles by pushing them beyond their normal workload. After inroading, the body sees the need to adapt to a higher level to protect itself against future high intensity activity. Your muscles must be fully recovered before each workout.

The rule is, if the TULs of 2 or more muscle groups digress twice in a row, it's time to add an extra, permanent rest day between workouts.

WORKOUT DATES AND LOAD TIMES			
EXERCISE	**5/10/2006**	**5/13/2006**	**5/16/2006**
BENCH PRESS	40 SECONDS	**30 SECONDS**	**28 SECONDS**
MILITARY PRESS	43 SECONDS	**35 SECONDS**	**30 SECONDS**
SHOULDER SHRUG	43 SECONDS	44 SECONDS	44 SECONDS
TRICEPS EXTENSION	40 SECONDS	42 SECONDS	45 SECONDS

Figure 11-10

Figure 11-10 shows that although progress was made on the shoulder shrug and triceps extension exercises, load times in the bench press and military press digressed consistently twice in a row; it's time to permanently add a day to rest and recovery time.

By keeping good records of workouts and checking progress often, you can determine your optimum rest and recovery time. The method to determine your recovery time is simple and the tools you need are on the workout sheet sets in the appendix of this book. Properly figuring your rest and recovery time can be broken into the following steps:

- Evaluate your progress/digress
- Flag exercises
- Add workout days if necessary

After each workout, fill out the set evaluation for the first working set of each exercise (Figure 11-11). The working set is the first set in which you lift the working weight.

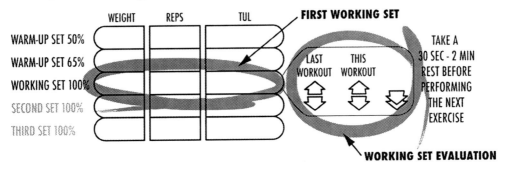

Figure 11-11

The working set evaluation is filled out by comparing the TUL of each muscle group on the current workout sheet with the last time those same muscle groups were worked. You will need to flip back in your records to find the last time you performed the current workout. For example, if you just finished performing the full-body workout sheet, you would flip back in your records to the last time you performed the full-body workout sheet.

Once you have both workout sheets in front of you it's time to compare them to determine if you need to add an extra rest and recovery day between workouts. There are 2 factors to consider when performing this task; the first is the progression or digression of the TULs of each exercise and the second is weather or not exercises have been *flagged*.

EVALUATE YOUR PROGRESS/DIGRESS

Evaluating the progress/digress of an exercise TULs is done by comparing the TULs of exercises on the past workout sheet with the TULs of exercises on the current workout sheet.

To make this comparison for one exercise, you will need the current workout sheet and the last workout sheet. Once you have the past and current workout sheets in front of you, transfer the progress/digress status of the last workout sheet onto the current workout sheet under the *LAST WORKOUT* area.

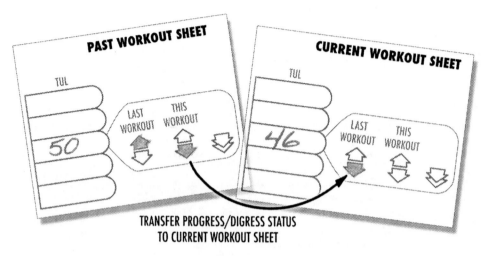

Figure 11-12

Figure 11-12 demonstrates the transfer of a past workout sheet's progress/digress onto a current workout sheet for a single muscle group/exercise.

Once you have checked either the up (progress) or down (digress) arrow under *LAST WORKOUT* on the current workout sheet, it's time to compare TULs between the 2 workouts. If the TUL for a given exercise on the current workout sheet is higher than the TUL for the same exercise on the last workout sheet then progress has been made and you should put a mark in the arrow pointing up under *THIS WORKOUT* on the current workout sheet.

If the TUL for a given exercise on the current workout sheet is lower than the TUL for the same exercise on the last workout sheet then either you have had a bad day in the gym or the muscles haven't had enough time to fully recover.

TRANSFER PROGRESS/DIGRESS STATUS
TO CURRENT WORKOUT SHEET

Figure 11-13

Figure 11-13 demonstrates that on the current workout sheet, the TUL of the current muscle group/exercise is lower than the TUL of the same muscle group/exercise on the last workout. This indicates that there has been a digression in lifting performance and the down arrow has been checked under THIS WORKOUT.

FLAG EXERCISES

Once you have compared your progress/digress for each exercise, its time to determine weather or not an additional rest and recovery day between workouts is necessary; this is done by *flagging* exercises. Flags are indicators that you have gained enough muscle mass or inroaded the muscles to the point where you can't fully recover between workouts without adding more recovery time.

A flag occurs if a given muscle group/exercise digresses twice in a row.

WORKOUT IS FLAGGED

Figure 11-14

Figure 11-14 illustrates that the muscle group/exercise has digressed twice in a row. This is indicated by marks in the down arrows under both LAST WORKOUT and THIS WORKOUT. In this case, the flag box should be marked for the muscle group/exercise.

ADD WORKOUT DAYS IF NECESSARY

After flagging muscle groups/exercises that have digressed twice in a row, it's time to determine if you need to add a permanent day to your rest and recovery time. This is done by comparing the number of flags on the past workout sheet with the number of flags on the current workout sheet. If there are 2 or more flags on the past workout sheet and 2 or more flags on the current workout sheet, it's time to add a permanent day of rest and recovery between strength training workouts to your regimen.

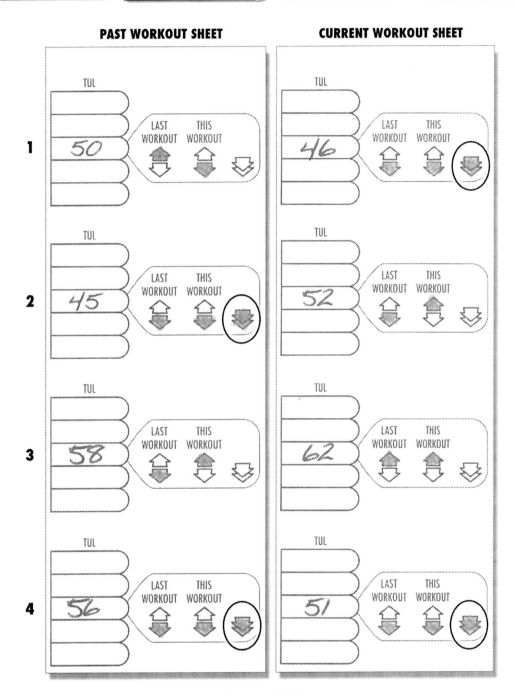

Figure 11-15

Figure 11-15 demonstrates that 2 muscle groups/exercises have been flagged on the current workout sheet (exercises 1 and 4) and that 2 muscle groups/exercises have been flagged on the past workout sheet (exercises 2 and 4). This indicates that a permanent rest and recovery day should be added between workouts.

If you are a beginner, the full body workout sheet and a 2-day recovery period is a great starting point. As you make progress and develop lean muscle mass, you will need to add recovery days. You can either add recovery days indefinitely or you can break your workout into multiple sessions with either the 2-day or 3-day breakout workout sheet sets. This will shorten time between gym visits and give each individual muscle group adequate recovery time.

With any workout, there is a level of energy depletion and entire body fatigue no matter which muscle groups are hit; thus 2 days of recovery time are absolutely required as a minimum between workouts.

The diagrams below illustrate recovery times naturally built into full body, 2-day breakout and 3-day breakout training regimens with 2 days of recovery time between workouts.

FULL BODY WORKOUT IN ONE SESSION

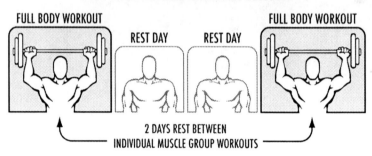

Figure 11-16

Figure 11-16 illustrates a full body workout regimen with 2 resting days between workouts. As muscle mass increases, additional recovery days should be added between workouts. When 5 recovery days between workouts is reached, breaking the body into 2 separate workout sessions becomes a good option.

WORKOUT BROKEN INTO TWO SESSIONS

Figure 11-17

Figure 11-17 illustrates a 2-day breakout workout regimen with 2 resting days between workouts. This system allows a full 5 days of rest for any single muscle group between workouts.

If biceps are worked during Workout 1 on Tuesday, and recovery time is kept at a 2 day minimum, biceps will not be worked again until the following Monday, allowing a full 5 recovery days between workouts. As muscle mass increases, additional recovery days should be added between workouts. When 8 recovery days between workouts is reached, breaking the body into 3 separate workout sessions becomes a good option.

WORKOUT BROKEN INTO THREE SESSIONS

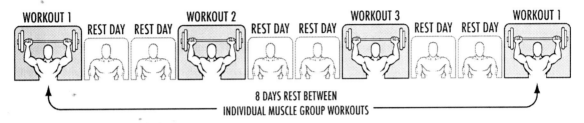

Figure 11-18

Figure 11-18 illustrates a 3-day breakout workout regimen with 2 resting days between workouts. This system allows a full 8 days of rest for any single muscle group between workouts.

If quads are worked during *Workout 1* and recovery time is kept at a 2-day minimum, quads will not be worked again for a full week and 2 days, allowing 8 days recovery time. As muscle mass increases, additional recovery days should be added between workouts; however it is not advised to break a workout regimen into more than three separate workouts.

Don't underestimate the power of rest and recovery time. Your muscles rebuild, adapt and become stronger between workouts. If you find that you have hit a plateau--your TULs to muscle failure do not increase, indicating that you don't seem to be getting stronger--try adding an additional day of rest and recovery time between workouts or try breaking your workout up into 2 days or 3 days. Often, you will break a plateau by merely allowing your body to more fully recover between workouts.

NOTE:

Total Human offers an excellent online tool to help you with your exercise records. For a reasonable, monthly fee, you can become a subscriber to Total Human: Virtual Trainer Pro. Virtual Trainer Pro acts like a real personal trainer by holding your hand during the strength training progress. Personal Trainer Pro issues custom workouts that you can print and take to the gym. Once you have performed these workouts, you can log your results into the system so that Virtual Trainer Pro can do all the calculations and issue your next workout. Your entire training journal is kept conveniently online. Virtual Trainer Pro also keeps track of all your body measurements and can even store pictures of you so that you can literally see your body adapt. With Virtual Trainer Pro, you will also have access to powerful exercise tutorials to help you be certain that you are performing every exercise with perfect form. For all these features and many more, check out Virtual Trainer Pro at www. totalhuman.com.

Working Out Step 6: Stay the Course

The last step is to make high intensity training a constant part of your life. Keep good records using the tools in the appendix of this book; review them often for motivation and encouragement. You can have the body you want. You now have the knowledge to improve your life-style, build strength and lean muscle mass and energize your body with the most effective strength training method in existence. It's never too late to begin working out; and if you have stopped, it's never too late to start again.

CHAPTER SUMMARY

APPLICATION

HIGH INTENSITY TRAINING: A STEP-BY-STEP GUIDE

- Adequate preparation for workouts involves; commitment, selection of routines, selection of exercises for muscle groups and selection of working weights for exercises.
- Each workout includes the following steps:
  - o Warm-up: a 5-10 minute aerobic warm-up
  - o Exercise: exercises should be performed with proper cadence and form
  - o Cool-down: a 5-10 minute aerobic cool-down
  - o Stretching: stretching exercises only need be performed for muscles worked during the workout
- A 30-second to 2-minute rest between exercise sets is an imperative part of working out.
- 2 warm-up sets should be performed before any exercise with 50% of the working weight for the first and 65% for the second.
- 1 set of exercise to muscle failure within 45 to 60 seconds is usually adequate to start the muscle building process.
- Multiple sets should only be performed if muscle failure occurs between 80 and 100% of the first set's time under load to muscle failure.
- Full rest and recovery should occur between workouts.

CHAPTER 12: CARDIOVASCULAR TRAINING

PRINCIPLES

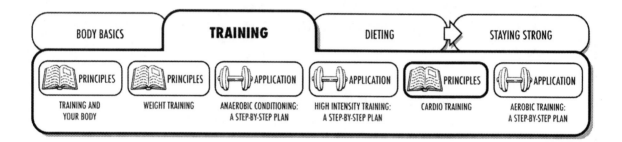

CHAPTER PREVIEW

Cardiovascular training burns calories by increasing the heart rate. High-impact cardiovascular exercise like running or stair stepping can have negative impact on joints. Low-impact exercise, like biking or walking, is less harmful to joints, tendons and ligaments.

CARDIOVASCULAR TRAINING

Cardiovascular training is an important component to a well-rounded exercise program. Cardiovascular training works muscles for an extended period of time and uses glycogen, fat and oxygen as fuel sources. This type of training includes such activities as walking, biking, distance running and cross-country running or hiking.

One of the main benefits of cardiovascular training is its ability to burn calories by increasing the heart rate. This can jumpstart your metabolism and burn more calories, even during resting periods.

Hitting the streets for a 20-minute run or bike ride 3 times a week is not the best way to burn the most possible calories. Running can be fun. People run for recreation. However, if your goal is to spend the least amount of time and get the most complete cardiovascular workout possible while limiting wear and tear on the body, it is best to understand how your aerobic and anaerobic systems respond to this type of exercise. Once you understand the principles, you should base your cardiovascular training around them.

HIGH INTENSITY VS. LOW INTENSITY CARDIOVASCULAR TRAINING

Cardiovascular exercises like running, elliptical, stair-stepping etc. train both the aerobic and anaerobic energy systems. The more intense the cardiovascular exercise, the more the anaerobic energy system is utilized; adversely, the less intense the cardiovascular exercise, the more the aerobic energy system is utilized.

High intensity exercise applies to cardiovascular training as well as anaerobic training. The whole idea behind high intensity training is to work the muscles using short bouts of high intensity activity. Sprinting is considered a high intensity exercise. Walking is considered a low intensity exercise. Like lifting heavy weights, sprinting spends energy in the muscles quickly and the body is forced to slow down or stop.

The most effective cardiovascular training method involves alternating between intervals of high intensity activity and lower intensity activity. This type of anaerobic/aerobic exercise is called *interval based* cardiovascular training. However, unlike maximal anaerobic strength training, cardiovascular exercise should not be maximal as this can be dangerous. The intensity of cardiovascular exercise should be dictated by your personal health and stamina. What is high intensity cardiovascular exercise to one person might be moderate in intensity to another.

When it comes to cardiovascular training, there is an age old dispute; in one corner you have the low-intensity people shouting *walk, don't run*; in the other corner you have the high intensity people yelling *run, don't walk;* so which is more effective, lower intensity walking or higher intensity running? Honestly, you are going to burn calories whether you choose to take a brisk walk for an hour every day or a good stiff bike ride for 20 minutes three times a week. The question is do you have an hour every day for a stroll?

The key to effective cardiovascular training is the amount of calories burned during a given time period. High intensity activities burn many times more calories than slow, drawn out, low-intensity activities. The heart is cardiac muscle and responds to high intensity stimulation much the same way skeletal muscle tissue does. Effective aerobic/anaerobic conditioning challenges the cardiovascular system with high intensity anaerobic activity for short bursts of time, followed by lower intensity intervals for short periods of time.

High Impact Cardiovascular Training

High impact training is any training style that exposes muscles, tendons, ligaments and joints to sudden high forces. Examples of high-impact cardiovascular training are running or sprinting. These activities, over time, take their toll on tendons, muscles and ligaments in the knees, lower legs and ankles.

Many people enjoy running; it has become a highly recreational activity. Races have become social events because they are fun. But it is important to remember the long-term costs of high-impact cardiovascular training exercise; ultimately, the detriments can outweigh the benefits.

A less harmful approach to cardiovascular training is the use of low impact exercises like biking or use of a cross-training machine. Using low impact exercise limits impact on tendons, ligaments, joints and muscles and essentially eliminates impact injury.

CHAPTER SUMMARY

PRINCIPLES

CARDIOVASCULAR TRAINING PRINCIPLES

- Effective cardiovascular training utilizes glycogen, oxygen and fat as fuels.
- Cardiovascular exercise includes activities like biking, running and hiking.
- High intensity cardiovascular training burns more calories in a shorter time period than low intensity aerobic training and better trains the cardiovascular system.
- Interval based cardiovascular training is the best way to burn calories using relatively short aerobic/anaerobic workouts.
- Interval based cardiovascular training involves alternating between high-intensity and lower-intensity exercise over a given time period.
- High impact exercise like running or sprinting can damage tendons, ligaments and joints over time.

CHAPTER 13: CARDIOVASCULAR TRAINING: A STEP-BY-STEP PLAN

APPLICATION

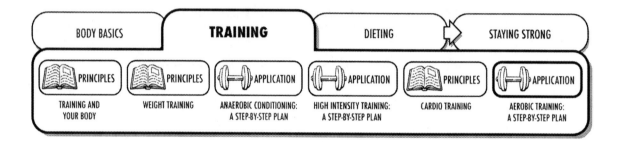

CHAPTER PREVIEW

Interval based cardio training is the best way to burn maximum calories in a short time period. Interval cardiovascular training is done by alternating high and mid intensity aerobic/anaerobic exercise during a cardiovascular workout.

CARDIO TRAINING STEP 1: CALCULATE YOUR MAXIMUM HEART RATE

With the use of highly effective interval based cardio workouts, you can stay lean and build cardiovascular strength with 2 to 3 workouts per week. Tracking your heart rate during a cardio workout is most effective. Most treadmills and gym cardio machines have a heart monitor built right onto the machine. If you are biking or hiking outside or working on a machine that does not have a heart rate monitor, you can buy one at most health stores or department stores.

To effectively use a heart monitor you must know your *maximum heart rate* (MHR). To figure your MHR, use the following, simple formula:

$$217 - (.85 \times [\text{your age}]) = [\text{MHR}]$$

For example, a 41-year old woman, we'll call her Jane, figures her maximum heart rate by putting her age into the formula as follows:

$$217 - (.85 \times 41) = 182.15$$

Jane's maximum heart rate is 182 (rounded down).

CARDIO TRAINING STEP 2: INTERVAL BASED CARDIO TRAINING

A proper cardio routine should be broken into intervals. Intervals are units of time during a cardio workout with varying levels of intensity.

Intensity is tracked by keeping an eye on your heart rate. After a 1 to 2 minute light aerobic warm-up, your goal should be to increase your heart rate to about 80% of your MHR and sustain that rate for 30-seconds to 1 minute; this is a high-intensity interval. After that time, you should decrease your pace and let your heart rate fall by about 20 beats per minute and sustain that pace for 1 minute; this is called a medium-intensity interval. This pattern should be repeated for a full 15 to 20 minutes—1 minute at high intensity, then 1 minute at medium intensity. After your 15 to 20-minute workout is complete, you should cool-down with a 1 to 2 minute walk.

Let's use Jane for an example. She steps onto a treadmill in her home to begin her aerobic routine. The first minute of her routine is spent warming up at a comfortable pace. She picks a good, brisk walking speed. After the first minute, she kicks it into high gear and keeps an eye on her heart rate. She's looking for a peak heart rate of around 80% percent of her MHR, that figures to about 145 beats per minute. After running flat-out for a short time, her heart rate finally reaches 145 beats per minute—that's a perfect heart rate. She continues running at that pace, keeping her heart rate steady at around 145 beats per minute for a full minute. After a minute she drops her pace back. Now she looks for her heart rate to drop 20 beats per minute to around 125 beats per minute. After slowing down, her heart rate decreases to 128—good enough. She stays at that pace for a full minute. Then POW, she takes off again, looking for that same peak heart rate at about 145 beats per minute. She keeps this pattern up for a full 20-minutes. When 20-minutes are up, she drops her pace to a comfortable walk and cools down for 1 to 2 minutes. She steps off the treadmill and towels off, feeling satisfied with a perfect cardiovascular workout.

Interval based cardiovascular training is only necessary 3 times a week to keep in good cardiovascular health and to raise the metabolism. It's a good idea to lock in a pattern for cardiovascular workout days and stick to it. You might reserve Monday, Wednesday and Friday mornings as cardio workout times.

If you decide to combine cardio and weight training in the same workout, be sure to perform your cardiovascular workout after weight training but before stretching. This will help hedge against injury and allow you to concentrate your energy on a good weight-training workout.

CHAPTER SUMMARY

APPLICATION

CARDIOVASCULAR TRAINGING: A STEP-BY-STEP PLAN

- Interval based cardiovascular training is the most efficient way to work the cardiovascular system.
- A calculation of the maximum heart rate is essential to interval based cardiovascular training.
- Interval based cardiovascular training includes raising the heart rate to about 80% of the maximum heart rate for 1 minute then lowering it by about 20 beats per minute for 1 minute. This cycle is repeated for 15 to 20 minutes.
- Three 15 to 20-minute interval based cardiovascular workouts a week are sufficient to raise the metabolism and keep the heart strong.
- If strength and cardiovascular training are to be performed on the same day, cardio training should be performed after strength training but before stretching.

MASTER CONCEPT 3: DIETING

| BODY BASICS | TRAINING | DIETING | STAYING STRONG |

- Calories are a measurement of energy.
- The proper amount of calories for any person can be figured using a simple formula.
- Calories are consumed in 3 ways.
    - The Basal Metabolic Rate
    - Activity level
    - Thermic effect of food
- Calories come from 3 sources.
    - Protein
    - Carbohydrates
    - Fats
- The 6 rules for a healthy diet are:
    - Eat a proper mix of proteins and carbohydrates.
    - Use the half-portion rule.
    - Watch when you eat.
    - Consume nutrient-rich calories.
    - Drink water.
    - Don't get discouraged.
- Reduced calorie dieters should carbohydrate load as part of training.

CHAPTER 14: MAINTAINING A HEALTHY DIET

PRINCIPLES

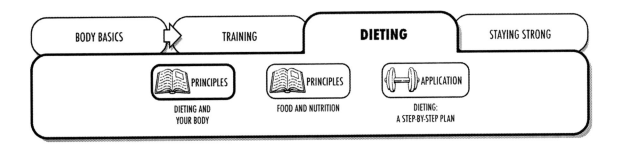

CHAPTER PREVIEW

Calories are a measurement of energy. The human body needs a minimum amount of calories to function each day. Calories are used in 3 ways; the basal metabolic rate, activity level and the thermic effect of food. A healthy diet and exercise work together to build and optimal body.

Diet Isn't a Four-letter Word

Building lean muscle mass has many benefits. But if you are looking for that shredded, buff look; if you are looking for a lean body build with attractive muscle tone then you have to watch your calorie intake. When it comes to leaning down to show off those hard earned muscles, a healthy diet is at least as important as weight and cardiovascular training.

Understanding the science behind basic nutrition, along with a little knowledge about the human metabolic system, greatly helps in putting together the right nutrition plan for you. A nutrition plan that incorporates foods you know and love is more effective than a fad diet that forces you to eat absurd amounts of meat and cheese or that takes you out of your eating comfort zone. Fad diets come and go because it is impossible to expect dieters to drastically change their eating habits for the rest of their lives.

You can eat the foods you love and still lose weight or maintain your optimum weight by understanding what food does once it is in your body. If you want to lose weight, you can modify your current eating habits to set you on a weight loss track if you start with the basics.

Calories Equal Energy

Energy is measured in units called calories. Energy comes in many forms and any block of energy, no matter what form, can be measured in calories. A gallon of gasoline contains about 31,000,000 calories. By definition, one calorie is the amount of energy it takes to raise the temperature of 1 gram of water 1 degree Celsius or 1.8 degrees Fahrenheit.

Calories of energy are taken from the food that you eat and used to power your body. Green vegetables are low in calories; ice cream is high in calories.

All foods are composites of three elements: fats, carbohydrates and proteins. Each of these elements contains a definite number of calories. There are 4 calories in 1 gram of carbohydrates, 4 calories in 1 gram of protein and 9 calories in 1 gram of fat. The total amount of energy in any food can be figured by adding the calories from each of these three elements.

A candy bar might have 10 grams of fat (10 grams @ 9 calories per gram = 90 calories), 41 grams of carbohydrates (41 grams @ 4 calories per gram = 164 calories) and 2 grams of protein (2 grams @ 4 calories per gram = 8 calories). If you add it all together, the total is 262 calories. If you could thoroughly burn the candy bar, enough energy would be generated to heat 262 grams of water by 1 degree Celsius or 1.8 degrees Fahrenheit. This is illustrated in Figure 14-1.

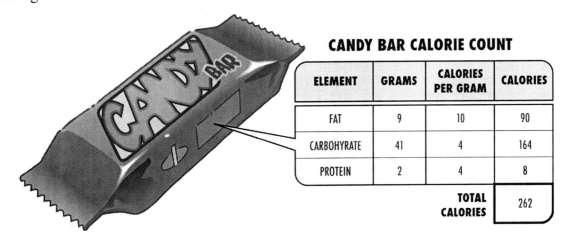

CANDY BAR CALORIE COUNT

ELEMENT	GRAMS	CALORIES PER GRAM	CALORIES
FAT	9	10	90
CARBOHYRATE	41	4	164
PROTEIN	2	4	8
		TOTAL CALORIES	262

Figure 14-1

Calories in food represent potential energy. Once calories are consumed in the form of food, they are burned by the metabolic system. Enzymes break carbohydrates down into glucose and other sugars. Fats are broken into glycerol and fatty acids. Proteins are broken into amino acids. Once broken down into these elements, they are put into the blood stream where they are either immediately used as energy or are mixed with oxygen to release stored energy.

How Many Calories Do You Need Each Day?

Each person requires a different number of calories each day. Many factors determine how many calories a person burns; some are height, weight, activity level and heart rate. All of these factors can be placed into three categories; basal metabolic rate, activity level and thermic effect of food.

Basal Metabolic Rate (BMR)

The basal metabolic rate is how many calories it takes to maintain the body at rest. It takes energy to run your heart, liver, lungs and kidneys and to fuel the processes that take place at a cellular level to maintain tissues. 70 to 80% of your daily calories are burned by your BMR. The BMR of a man is usually higher than that of a woman. You can calculate your BMR by using the Harris-Benedict formula (Figure 14-2).

HARRIS–BENEDICT BASAL METABOLIC RATE FORMULA	
MEN	66 + (6.23 x BODY WEIGHT IN LBS.) + (12.7 x HEIGHT IN INCHES) - (6.8 x AGE IN YEARS)
WOMEN	655 + (4.35 x BODY WEIGHT IN LBS.) + (4.7 x HEIGHT IN INCHES) - (4.7 x AGE IN YEARS)

Figure 14-2

A 34-year old man who is 185 lbs and 70 inches tall would figure his BMR by using the following formula:

$$BMR = 66 + (6.23 \times 185) + (12.7 \times 70) - (6.8 \times 34) = 1876.35$$

In this example the man burns 1876.35 calories of energy at rest every day.

ACTIVITY LEVEL

Activity level includes any physical activity performed during the day; walking, running, cleaning the house, washing the car and changing stations on the remote control all take effort and are a part of the activity level category. Any activity above lying in bed counts. Activity level is the second highest calorie-burning category.

Exercise fits into this category. How many calories are burned during an activity depends on the weight of the person performing the action. Figure 14-3 illustrates some average projections of how many calories are burned while performing various activities, categorized by body weight.

CALORIE BURN FOR ONE HOUR OF ACTIVITY

ACTIVITY	BODY WEIGHT		
	130 LBS	155 LBS	190 LBS
HIGH IMPACT AEROBICS	413	493	604
LOW IMPACT AEROBICS	295	352	431
BACKPACKING	413	493	604
BASKETBALL	472	563	690
STATIONARY BICYCLING	413	493	604
CLEANING THE HOUSE	207	246	302
FOOTBALL	472	563	690
GOLF	236	281	345
HIGH INTENSITY WEIGHT LIFTING	354	422	518

Figure 14-3

NOTE: The numbers represent calories per hour

In the morning, a man of 190 pounds attends an hour-long low impact aerobics class burning 431 calories. He spends 2 hours that same day cleaning his house 604 calories (302 x 2). Both activities add up to 1,035 calories.

Your lifestyle has everything to do with how many calories you burn each day. Are you an active person? Or do you tend to be more sedentary? You can quickly get an idea of your daily activity calorie burn by comparing your lifestyle to the chart below. Figure 14-4 has 5 life-style categories, ranging from sedentary to extra active. Each category is associated with a percentage modifier for both men and women. Your daily activity calorie burn can be calculated by multiplying the percentage modifier associated with your life-style by your BMR.

ACTIVITY LEVEL	DESCRIPTION	MODIFIER
SEDENTARY	LITTLE TO NO EXERCISE	.2
LIGHTLY ACTIVE	LIGHT EXERCISE SPORTS 1-3 DAYS A WEEK	.375
MODERATELY ACTIVE	MODERATE EXERCISE SPORTS 3-5 DAYS A WEEK	.55
VERY ACTIVE	HARD EXERCISE SPORTS 6-7 DAYS A WEEK	.725
EXTRA ACTIVE	HARD DAILY EXERCISE SPORTS AND A PHYSICAL JOB	.9

Figure 14-4

A man--a computer programmer--looks at the above chart and categorizes himself as lightly active. After figuring his BMR at 1876.35 calories per day, he takes the associated percentage modifier from the lightly active life-style category and multiplies it by his BMR as follows.

$$1876.35 \times .375 = 703.63$$

His average daily activity calorie burn is 703.63 calories.

THERMIC EFFECT OF FOOD

The act of eating and digesting food takes energy. It takes energy to chew the food. The digestive and intestinal system needs energy to break the food down. Calories burned by the metabolic system can be figured by taking the total number of daily calories consumed and multiplying it by .1 (10% of the total daily calorie intake = thermal effect of food).

A man consumes 2500 calories in one day. The thermic burn calculation is used to figure his caloric burn:

$$2500 \times .1 = 250 \text{ calories}$$

In the process of breaking food down, the man's metabolic system burns 250 calories.

A LIVING EXAMPLE

By adding all three calorie burning systems together, the total amount of daily calories burned can be calculated. Figure 14-5 demonstrates that a 34-year old man who weighs 185 pounds has a BMR of 1876.35 calories. He is a computer programmer who lives a lightly active life-style, so his activity level calorie burn is 703.63. On the average, he consumes 2500 calories, so his average thermal calorie burn is 250 calories per day. The sum of these 3-calorie burning systems equals 2829.98—the total number of calories burned by this man in one day.

TOTAL CALORIE BURN FOR 1 DAY

CALORIE BURN FACTOR	FORMULA	CALORIE BURN
BASAL METABOLIC RATE	$66 + (6.23 \times 185) + 12.7 \times 70) - (6.8 \times 34) =$	1876.35
ACTIVITY LEVEL	$1876.35 \times .375 =$	703.63
THERMIC EFFECT OF FOOD	$2500 \times .1 =$	250
	TOTAL CALORIES CONSUMED	2829.98

Figure 14-5

A CALORIE IS A CALORIE IS A CALORIE

Does it matter where calories come from? Are calories from fat more potent or harder to burn than calories from carbohydrates or protein? The answers to these questions can be rolled into one simple statement: when it comes to weight control, a calorie is a calorie is a calorie. A calorie is nothing more than a measurement of energy. Your body needs a certain amount of energy to function. It doesn't care where this energy comes from, as long as it is in place and ready to use. If your body requires 2,500 calories a day to maintain its daily groove, it will spend those 2,500 calories with no consideration as to where they came from.

When it comes to healthy nutrition, there is a difference. It is healthier to consume calories from carbohydrates and proteins than from fat. Too much fat can cause health problems including high cholesterol and heart disease. However, fat is an important requirement to your body's nutritional health. Fat helps your body absorb vitamins you ingest from food. 15% to 20% of your daily calorie intake should be from fat. Hence, if you consume 2,500 calories in a day, 375 to 500 of those calories should be from fat.

105

UNHEALTHY DIETS

There are many diet fads that claim to melt pounds off at an incredible rate. Some tout 10 to 15 pound drops per week. The truth is if you loose more than 1 to 2 pounds in one week's time, you are either loosing water weight or going about dieting in an unhealthy manner and losing muscle mass as well as fat. Watch out for big promises in the dieting world; they might involve diuretics, which flush your system of fluids. They might prescribe drugs (like caffeine) that boost your heart rate.

Low carbohydrate diets work by dropping the intake of carbohydrates to an insanely low calorie level. By using this method, scale weight will go down; however, by lowering your carbohydrate intake, you are effectively increasing your fat intake, in many cases, above 15% to 20% of your daily calorie intake. You are risking health problems that may include high cholesterol and heart disease.

Another problem with low carb-diets is that energy is sapped, making workouts in the gym or on the track much less effective. Carbohydrates provide the most immediate source of body energy. Pounds lost on low-carb diet plans without exercise often slingshot right back onto the body. If your plan is to lose weight with a combination of exercise and dieting (the most effective method), a low-carb diet is not the best option.

DIETING AND EXERCISE WORK TOGETHER

Dieting is a great way to drop a few dress sizes; but pounds lost by dieting without exercise are less supported by your body's natural metabolism. If you go on a crash diet and lose 10 pounds while not building the muscle mass to heighten your body's natural metabolism, it is likely that you will quickly gain that 10 pounds back. You will miss out on a key element of optimal and permanent weight control.

Crash diets cause fat loss, but they also cause muscle loss. A pound of muscle burns up to 50 calories per day at rest; a pound of fat burns only 3 calories per day at rest. If you lose 10 pounds of bodyweight and 5 of those pounds are muscle, up to 250 calories less are burned per day. This makes permanent weight loss difficult.

On the other hand, if you work out regularly but insist on getting a super-sized combo meal three times a day (that's about 3,000 calories) and eating a bowl of ice cream every night before you go to bed, you may increase your strength and even your aerobic stamina, but you are not going to lose weight.

About 3,500 calories makes up 1 pound of body fat. If you consume the exact amount of calories your body needs each day, you will maintain your weight. If you consume 3,500 more calories than your body needs to function in several days, you will gain 1 pound of fat. Inversely, if you consume 3,500 fewer calories than your body needs in the same time period, you will loose 1 pound of body fat.

If a 34 year old, 185-pound man wants to lose 2 pounds of body fat in one week, he could drop his calorie intake and boost his exercise accordingly to do so. To loose 2 pounds of body fat, he will have to burn 7,000 (3,500 x 2) extra calories throughout the week. Figures 14-6 through 14-8 show how he can accomplish this.

MAN'S PROFILE

SEX	WEIGHT	HEIGHT	AGE	BMR	LIFE-STYLE
MALE	185 LBS.	70 IN.	34	1,876.35	MODERATELY ACTIVE (.375 PERCENTAGE MODIFIER)

Figure 14-6

	SUN	MON	TUE	WED	THU	FRI	SAT
BMR	1,876.35	1,876.35	1,876.35	1,876.35	1,876.35	1,876.35	1,876.35
MODERATE ACTIVITY LEVEL (.375 MODIFIER)	703.63	703.63	703.63	703.63	703.63	703.63	703.63
THERMAL EFFECT OF FOOD	160	160	160	160	160	160	160
TOTAL CALORIES BURNED	2,739.98	2,739.98	2,739.98	2,739.98	2,739.98	2,739.98	2,739.98
TOTAL CALORIES BURNED	1,600	1,600	1,600	1,600	1,600	1,600	1,600
DAILY CALORIE DEFICIT	1,139.98	1,139.98	1,139.98	1,139.98	1,139.98	1,139.98	1,139.98

Figure 14-7

TOTAL WEEKLY CALORIES BURNED	19,179.9
TOTAL WEEKLY CALORIES CONSUMED	11,200
TOTAL WEEKLY CALORIE DEFICIT	7,979.86
POUNDS LOST	2.27

Figure 14-8

The above tables illustrate that a man with a moderately active lifestyle and a reasonable diet of 1,600 calories per day can lose 2.27 pounds per week. His total calories burned for the week (19,179.9) minus his total calories consumed for the week (11,200) equals his calorie deficit for the week (7,979.86). His total calorie deficit (7,979.86) divided by 3,500 (calories in 1 pound of fat) equals his total fat loss in pounds (2.27 pounds).

19,179.9 (calories burned) – 11,200 (calories consumed) = 7,979 (Total calorie deficit)

7,979 (total calorie deficit)/3,500 (calories in 1 fat pound) = 2.27

(pounds of fat lost in 1 week)

This is an excellent example of how dieting and exercise work together to help melt away pounds of fat.

NOTE:

There are more accurate ways to calculate your daily caloric need. The methods in this book are meant to be quick and convenient. Using these formulas, you can determine a starting point and work from there. Once you have a starting point, you can fine-tune it by adjusting your activity level and diet until you have tailored a regimen to help you attain your weight loss goals.

CHAPTER SUMMARY

PRINCIPLES

DIETING AND YOUR BODY

- Energy is measured in units called calories.
- There are 3 calorie burning systems in the human body:
    - o The basal metabolic rate
    - o The activity level
    - o The thermic effect of food
- Calories are burned indiscriminately by the body, no matter what source they come from
- Exercise raises the metabolism and supports weight loss from dieting

CHAPTER 15: FOOD AND NUTRITION

PRINCIPLES

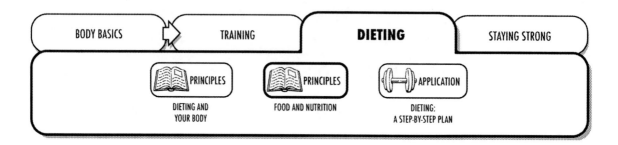

```
BODY BASICS          TRAINING          DIETING          STAYING STRONG

         PRINCIPLES          PRINCIPLES          APPLICATION

      DIETING AND        FOOD AND NUTRITION        DIETING:
      YOUR BODY                                A STEP-BY-STEP PLAN
```

CHAPTER PREVIEW

Calories come from 3 sources, protein, carbohydrate and fat. Protein contains essential amino acids. There are 2 types of carbohydrates, simple carbohydrates and complex carbohydrates. Fats are essential but should be consumed in moderation and in the correct proportions.

ALL CALORIES ARE NOT CREATED EQUAL

Every calorie should count in a nutritional sense. You can consume a daily allotment of 2,000 calories in ice cream, but you will be hungry for most of the day and risk your health with such a plan. A better approach is to use healthy sources of energy including a balanced diet of fruits, whole grains, vegetables, lean meats, poultry, fish, low fat dairy, nuts and plenty of water.

60% of your daily calorie intake should be in the form of carbohydrates, 20 to 25% from protein and 15 to 20% from fats. Carbohydrates are the primary source of fuel during training sessions and if you are not getting an adequate supply, you will not be able to perform at your best during workouts.

The best way to know where your calories come from is to check the nutritional information on the packaging of everything you eat. The main three nutritional facts to look for are how many calories come from fat, from carbohydrates and from protein. Figure 15-1 illustrates a typical daily eating log.

BREAKFAST

FOOD ITEM	CALORIES	CARBS	PROTEIN	FAT
4 SLICES OF BACON	146	0	32	124
2 EGGS	148	4	25	50
1 GLASS OF WATER	0	0	0	0

LUNCH

FOOD ITEM	CALORIES	CARBS	PROTEIN	FAT
CHICKEN FILLET SANDWICH	265	155	96	294
FRUIT COCKTAIL	76	80	4	1
1 CAN OF SODA	0	0	0	0

DINNER

FOOD ITEM	CALORIES	CARBS	PROTEIN	FAT
SPAGHETTI	197	159	27	9
SPAGHETTI SAUCE	143	82	14	52
2 SLICES GARLIC BREAD	186	83	17	96
1 CAN OF SODA	0	0	0	0

SNACK

FOOD ITEM	CALORIES	CARBS	PROTEIN	FAT
CANDY BAR	270	164	8	100

TOTALS

CALORIES	1431		
CARBS	727	DAY'S CARB %	51
PROTEIN	223	DAY'S PROTEIN %	16
FAT	726	DAY'S FAT %	51

Figure 15-1

This example does not reflect an ideal diet; it shows that the total calories consumed are 1,431; that is not many calories. A safe minimum calorie threshold is 1,500 for men and 1,000 for women. Though the overall calorie count is low and would induce weight loss, 51% of the total calorie intake is from fat—much more than the recommended 15% to 20%. Protein should be boosted from a paltry 16% to between 20% and 25%. Carbohydrates should be boosted from 51% to 60%.

CARBOHYDRATES

Carbohydrates are your prime source of energy and come from such foods as breads, cereals, rice and pasta. These foods offer a rich supply of vitamins, minerals and necessary fiber to your diet. Fast, ready energy is the role of carbohydrates. Carbohydrates are quickly converted to glucose, which flows through the blood stream and into the muscles. Glucose is a sugar that is the primary energy source for your body.

All carbohydrates are not the same; there are 2 kinds of carbohydrates, simple carbohydrates and complex carbohydrates.

Simple carbohydrates are sugars that can be absorbed into the blood stream directly through the intestinal lining and are rapidly converted into glucose. How rapidly? If you drink a can of soda, glucose enters your bloodstream at about 30 calories per minute; that's quick.

When the blood is flooded with glucose at this rate, the body has to react chemically. With the rapid rise of glucose levels in the blood, the pancreas produces higher levels of insulin to keep glucose levels from rising too high. Insulin often does its job a little too well and pushes glucose levels below where they should be after 3 or 4 hours. Low glucose levels trigger a surge of adrenaline into the blood. And so you ride a rollercoaster of hormonal peaks and valleys.

Spikes and lows of insulin and adrenaline can affect your mood and fluctuate your performance throughout the day. Another function of insulin is to convert excess glucose into fat. With this in mind, do you really want extra glucose flowing through your system?

Foods that contain simple carbohydrates usually do not contain much nutritional value. Some examples are candy, soda-pop, cake, sweets and white bread. Stay away from simple carbohydrates as much as possible.

Complex carbohydrates, commonly known as starches, must be broken down by your digestive system into glucose to use as energy. It takes much longer to break down starches. Glucose from complex carbohydrates enters your bloodstream at the rate of about 2 calories per minute.

With complex carbohydrates you don't experience the spikes and lows in blood sugar as with simple carbohydrates. Glucose levels remain consistent and less is converted into fat.

Foods containing complex carbohydrates usually have other nutritional value as well. Some examples of foods rich in complex carbohydrates are oats, whole grains, wheat bread, corn, rice, vegetables, potatoes and plantains. These foods provide a wide range of vitamins and minerals as well as complex carbohydrates.

PROTEINS

The human body can't survive on carbohydrates alone. Carbohydrates act as energy for your cells; but proteins contain the building blocks of those cells. Each cell in your body survives by perpetually growing and maintaining its health. Proteins contain the materials that allow this process to occur.

Just like carbohydrates, all proteins are not created equal. A protein is a combination of different amino acids. There are many kinds of amino acids, each with a different function; but all act as building blocks for cellular health.

There are 2 different categories of proteins, complete proteins and incomplete proteins. Complete proteins contain every essential amino acid that your body needs for cellular growth and health. Incomplete proteins are weak in some amino acids and strong in others.

Cells must receive an adequate amount of all essential amino acids each day. Foods containing complete proteins are typically in the meat category; some examples are poultry, eggs, egg substitutes, beef and fish.

Many fruits and vegetables are rich in proteins as well but usually contain incomplete proteins. Soybeans, nuts and legumes are a great source of non-animal protein. When combined properly with the right fruits and vegetables, they will give your body its daily allotment of essential amino acids.

FATS

Fats are an essential part of your body's health and must be consumed daily. There are two types of fats, saturated fats and unsaturated fats. Saturated fats are fats that solidify at room temperature--lard, shortening, butter. Unsaturated fats remain in liquid form at room temperature--vegetable oils. Most food sources contain a combination of both kinds of fats. It is believed that unsaturated fats are healthier and easier on your body than saturated fats.

Fats are broken down and transported into the blood stream. Once in the blood, they are either used as energy or stored for later use as fat reserves. Fat is an excellent energy source. There are twice the calories in one gram of fat as in one gram of carbohydrates. But beware; if you consume too much fat, your body will store it away for a rainy day in the form of a potbelly, blubbery thighs or love handles.

To cut fat entirely out of your diet is a mistake that can cost you your health; there are essential fatty acids that your body requires on a daily basis. Some vitamins like A, D, E and

K are fat-soluble. This means that without fat, your body is unable to absorb these essential vitamins.

Though fat is an important part of your diet, it is wise to watch your fat intake. Keeping fats down to 15 – 20% of your daily calorie consumption is a good rule. Your body will have enough fat to utilize fat soluble vitamins and provide the essential fatty acids your body needs without packing away too much into reserves.

Avoid saturated fats as much as possible. Good sources of essential fats are found in avocados, nuts, canola/sunflower/olive oils and fish such as fresh tuna and salmon.

GOOD FOODS AND FOODS TO BE EATEN IN MODERATION

Now that you understand the purpose of carbohydrates, proteins and fats, the next question is how should you eat? Figure 15-2 presents many good options, in both the carbohydrate and protein categories. By sticking to low-fat dairy and lean meats like poultry and fish, you will effectively limit fat in your diet.

CARBOHYDRATES		PROTEINS	
GOOD FOODS	EAT IN MODERATION	GOOD FOODS	EAT IN MODERATION
WHOLEGRAIN PASTA	CANDY	SKINLESS CHICKEN	ANY FATTY MEAT
BAKED POTATOES	LIGHT CHOCOLATES	FIRM FISH (TROUT, SALMON)	EXCESS BUTTER OR MARGARINE
RICE	WHITE BREAD	LEAN ROUND STEAK	FRIED FOOD
WHOLEGRAIN BREAD	SUGAR SODAS	LEAN GROUND BEEF (IN MODERATION)	EXCESS SALAD DRESSING
BLACK BEANS	SUGAR PUNCH	LEAN CHUCK ARM	PIZZA
PINTO BEANS	SNACK CAKES	LEAN SIRLOIN	FATTY HAMBURGERS
KIDNEY BEANS	PIZZA	PORK CHOPS	MOST FAST FOOD
BANANAS	MOST FAST FOOD	PORK TENDER LOIN	SHELLFISH
APPLES	FROSTING	PORK CENTER LOIN	EGG YOLKS
BRAN CEREALS	CREAM	HAM	
PEAS	CHEESE	VEAL (ALL CUTS EXCEPT GROUND)	
CORN	MAPLE SYRUP	LAMB ROAST	
BROCCOLI		LAMB CHOPS	
RAISINS		LAMB LOIN	
COUSCOUS		LAMB FORE SHANKS	
GREEN SALAD		TURKEY (LIGHT/DARK, NO SKIN)	
		SOY BEANS	
		LEGUMES	
		NUTS (1 HANDFUL A DAY)	
		TUNA FISH	

Figure 15-2

CHAPTER SUMMARY

PRINCIPLES

FOOD AND NUTRITION

- Calories come from the following 3 nutrition sources:
  - o Fats
  - o Proteins
  - o Carbohydrates
- Essential amino acids mainly come from proteins.
- Fats are necessary to breakdown certain vitamins.
- Carbohydrates are the body's main source of energy
- Fats should constitute 15 to 20% of an effective daily diet.

Chapter 16: Dieting: A Step-by-step Plan

Application

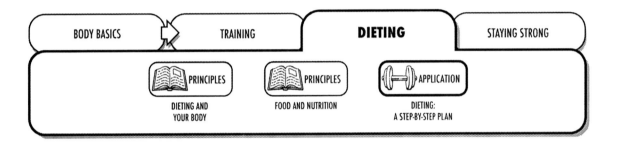

Chapter Preview

Calculating daily caloric need is the starting point to implementing an effective weight-loss dieting plan. There are 6 rules of good dieting, sensible protein and carbohydrate balance, eating small meals throughout the day to keep the metabolism going, eating nutrient rich foods, drinking water and not getting discouraged. Dieters should load up on carbohydrates before training sessions.

FIGURE YOUR DAILY CALORIC NEED

The entry point to effective dieting is in calculating how many calories per day you need to maintain your current weight. This is done by calculating a base daily calorie burn rate using the Harris-Benedict formula and fine tuning that base by adjusting your calorie intake and keeping track of your scale weight.

A worksheet is provided in the appendix of this book to help you calculate your base daily caloric need. The worksheet breaks the process into 4 easy steps.

Step 1: Calculate your Basal Metabolic Rate

The first step on the caloric need worksheet helps you to calculate your basal metabolic rate.

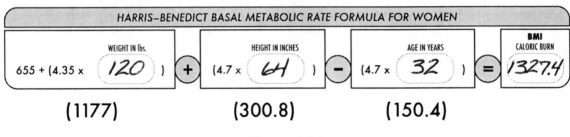

HARRIS–BENEDICT BASAL METABOLIC RATE FORMULA FOR WOMEN

655 + (4.35 x *120*) + (4.7 x *64*) − (4.7 x *32*) = BMI CALORIC BURN *1327.4*

(1177) (300.8) (150.4)

Figure 16-1

The Harris-Benedict formula has been broken into 3 parts for easy calculation of your BMR. Using the daily caloric need worksheet, first, write your weight, height and age in the provided boxes (Figure 16-1). Make sure you use the box set for your sex. Once you have written these 3 numbers, work the calculations in each gray box and write the results below the calculations. After completing the 3 calculations, subtract the third from the sum of the first and second to get your BMR.

The example formula above from the daily caloric need sheet shows that a 120 lb, 5'4" (64"), 32-year-old woman has a basal metabolic rate of 1327.4 calories per day.

STEP 2: CALCULATE YOUR ACTIVITY LEVEL

Your activity level is determined by using the *Figure Your Activity Level Caloric Burn* portion of the daily caloric need worksheet (Figure 16-2).

2. CALCULATE YOUR ACTIVITY LEVEL CALORIC BURN

ACTIVITY LEVEL	DESCRIPTION	MODIFIER
SEDENTARY	LITTLE TO NO EXERCISE	.2
LIGHTLY ACTIVE	LIGHT EXERCISE SPORTS 1-3 DAYS A WEEK	.375
MODERATELY ACTIVE	MODERATE EXERCISE SPORTS 3-5 DAYS A WEEK	.55
VERY ACTIVE	HARD EXERCISE SPORTS 6-7 DAYS A WEEK	.725
EXTRA ACTIVE	HARD DAILY EXERCISE SPORTS AND A PHYSICAL JOB	.9

BMR | ACTIVITY MODIFIER | ACTIVITY CALORIC BURN

$$1327.4 \times .375 = 497.8$$

Figure 16-2

Write your BMR in the provided space. Reference the activity level modifier table and write the modifier into the *Activity Modifier* space in the calculation. Multiply your BMR by the modifier to get your *Activity Caloric Burn*. This number is an estimation of how many calories you burn per day as a result of activity.

STEP 3: CALCULATE YOUR THERMIC EFFECT OF FOOD

The *thermic effect of food* calculation on the daily caloric need worksheet is based on your BMR plus your activity caloric burn. The worksheet helps you calculate your thermic effect of food as if you are consuming an ideal number of calories or the exact caloric need of your BMR plus your activity level. Your true thermic effect of food is based on the actual number of calories consumed, not the BMR plus activity level; but the worksheet calculation gives you a good approximation.

3. CALCULATE YOUR THERMIC EFFECT OF FOOD FOR BMI AND ACTIVITY LEVEL

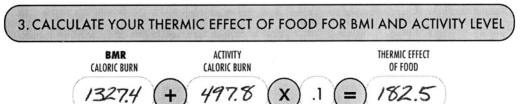

BMR CALORIC BURN | ACTIVITY CALORIC BURN | THERMIC EFFECT OF FOOD

$$1327.4 + 497.8 \times .1 = 182.5$$

Figure 16-3

Your thermic effect of food is 10% of the total calories consumed per day. To figure this, use the calculation found in step 3 of the daily caloric need worksheet (Figure 16-3). Write your *BMR* in the provided box. Write your *activity caloric burn* in the provided box. Add the two numbers and multiply the sum by .1 to get your estimated *thermic effect of food.*

STEP 4: CALCULATE YOUR TOTAL CALORIC NEED

To calculate your total daily caloric need, write your BMR, activity and thermic effect of food in the provided boxes and add the three numbers together (Figure 16-4). The sum is your total daily caloric need.

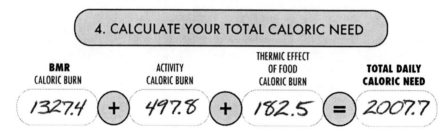

4. CALCULATE YOUR TOTAL CALORIC NEED

BMR CALORIC BURN		ACTIVITY CALORIC BURN		THERMIC EFFECT OF FOOD CALORIC BURN		TOTAL DAILY CALORIC NEED
1327.4	+	497.8	+	182.5	=	2007.7

Figure 16-4

We can conclude from the above example that a 32-year-old woman of 120 lbs. with a lightly active lifestyle burns 2007.7 calories a day to maintain her current weight.

This method helps you to estimate how many calories it takes to maintain your current weight at your current activity level. The formulas on the daily caloric need worksheet are general. You will need to fine-tune these numbers for your own body.

STEP 5: FINE TUNING

Once you have worked the calculations on the daily caloric requirement worksheet, it's time to fine-tune the numbers. This is done by performing the following steps:

1. Weigh yourself on a bathroom scale and write your weight down.
2. Keep a detailed log of every calorie you consume for 7 days. Try to stay within the daily caloric requirement on your worksheet.
3. At the end of 7 days, total the calories and divide them by 7; this will give you your average calorie intake per day.
4. Check your weight on a bathroom scale at the end of the week.
   a. If your weight remains the same you have correctly determined how many calories you can consume and maintain your current weight.

   b. If your weight goes down, add 500 calories a day to your daily intake and check your weight again in another week. After the second week of calorie tracking, you should be pretty close to your ideal calorie intake per day to maintain your current weight.

   c. If your weight goes up, you are consuming more calories than you need to maintain your current weight. Drop your daily calorie intake by 500 calories a day and weigh again after another week. You should be pretty close to the daily calories needed to maintain your current weight.

5. If your goal is to lose weight, once you have discovered how many calories you need to maintain your current weight, drop your daily calorie intake by 500 to 1000 calories a day. You will drop pounds at a healthy 1 to 2 pound rate per week.

1 pound of body fat contains about 3,500 calories. By dropping your calorie intake by 500 calories a day, you are denying your body 1 pound of fuel in the form of fat per week (500 x 7 = 3500).

The body needs a certain amount of calories to function; it is possible to drop your calorie intake below its minimum safety level. Men should consume no less than 1,500 calories per day; women, no less than 1,000. Always be sure to consume these minimums in calories unless you are under the supervision of a doctor.

With fluctuations in your weight and increases in lean muscle mass, your body's calorie needs will change. The more weight you lose, the harder it will be to lose weight. You will hit plateaus along the way. Don't become discouraged. When you reach a plateau, recalculate your maintenance calorie level as outlined in the steps above and drop your calorie intake by 500 calories per day.

21 Days To a Fat-burning Diet

You don't have to count every single calorie you eat on an ongoing basis. It is a good idea to count calories for a short period of time (a couple of weeks) to get an idea of how many calories you consume each day and to understand how many calories are in food.

You don't need to drastically change the foods you eat to lose weight. Many fad diets ask for gigantic shifts in eating habits to lose weight fast. Such shifts can be difficult to maintain. Many dieters tend to move from fad diet to fad diet trying to find one that works; the only consistency in this method is change.

A fat burning diet can be sustained by developing good dieting habits. Habits are behaviors that are developed over time with repetition and consistency. Psychological studies have shown that it takes 21 days to break a bad habit and replace it with a good one. Listed below are 7 dieting rules to help you lose weight. Set a goal at this moment to follow these rules for 21 days and turn them into habits.

RULE 1: PROTEIN AND CARBOHYDRATE BALANCE

Dividing calorie intake by the three nutritional categories--carbohydrates, proteins and fats--does not have to be complicated. Sure, you can read the nutritional labels of everything you eat and write detailed notes on exactly where every calorie comes from, that method works great. But there is an easier way. Divide any meal you prepare into 3 equal parts, 1 part protein and 2 parts carbohydrates.

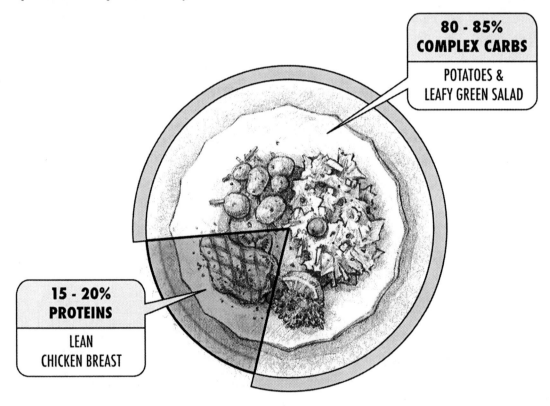

Figure 16-5

Think of your plate as a pie chart as you pile it with food (Figure 16-5). 15 to 20% should be proteins. The remaining 80 to 85% should be in the form of complex carbohydrates. Your fat intake will be covered properly if you stick to lean meats and low-fat salad dressings and oils. Protein per meal, if taken in the form of meat, should be one serving about the size

of your palm--1 medium sized pork chop, a 4 oz steak or 2 eggs. A simple way to balance nutritional value is to take the protein serving size and eat about twice as much complex carbohydrate rich food in the form of fruits, vegetables and whole grains.

RULE 2: THE HALF-PORTION RULE

Portion-size is one of the main considerations when it comes to a fat burning diet. You would be surprised at how little food can satisfy you. The less you eat, the less can be converted into fat reserves.

Use the rule of halves. When you begin to pile a plate with food, try restricting the amount of food to half of what you would regularly serve yourself. After finishing a plate of half-portions, think about how you feel. Do you feel satisfied? Do you feel hungry? Do you really need seconds? You might be surprised. Over time, by using the half-portion rule, your stomach will shrink and it will take less and less to be satisfied.

On the other hand, don't starve yourself. If you finish a plate of half-sized portions and you still feel hungry, take seconds; but try to stay away from meats and proteins. Pile your plate with seconds of vegetables to satisfy your appetite.

RULE 3: WATCH WHEN YOU EAT

An effective dieter does not deprive his body of essential nutrients. To diet safely, you must eat enough food to keep your metabolism humming on an ongoing basis. Meals should be spread throughout the day so your body is always working and you don't get hungry. Allow yourself three full meals and no more than 2 snacks. You should eat a good breakfast, lunch and dinner at standard meal times. Up to 2 low-fat snacks are allowed if spread evenly between meals. You might eat an 8 oz container of low fat yogurt at about 10:00 right between your breakfast and lunch.

RULE 4: CONSUME NUTRIENT-RICH CALORIES

For proteins, stick to lean meats like chicken, turkey lean beef and lean pork. Watch out for fatty hamburger, fried foods and salad dressings.

Carbohydrates should come from wholesome, nutritional vegetables and fruits. Find ways to substitute simple sugars with complex carbs. Substitute whole grain bread for white bread and limit candies and sweets to a minimum. You can switch from white tortillas to wheat tortillas; the browner the breads the better. Eat plenty of leafy green vegetables like lettuce and spinach. You can't eat enough wholesome vegetables like carrots, peppers, artichokes and celery.

Cut sugar sodas from your diet entirely. If you just can't live without a can of soda, opt for diet drinks. One can of sugar cola contains about 200 calories; one can of sugar free cola contains 0 calories. The average man drinks 2 cans of sugar soda a day--almost a quarter of his daily caloric need is wasted on simple sugars. This spikes the glucose levels and saps energy.

RULE 5: DRINK WATER

Water makes up about 60% of your body's composition. Each day you lose much of your water through urine, sweat and moisture exhaled from your lungs. At rest about 40 ounces of water a day is lost; that is about a third of a gallon. If you spend a day working hard out in the hot sun, you can loose twice that amount. Water is essential to your body's ability to function.

At a minimum, drink 8 cups of water a day or 64 ounces. That is half a gallon. The more the better is the rule. A good tip is to drink a tall glass of water before every meal to take the edge off your appetite and to help keep your portion sizes down to an acceptable level.

RULE 6: DON'T GET DISCOURAGED

These 5 rules are not hard and fast. Flexibility is deliberately built into them. Much of dieting comes down to good common sense. Only put good nutritional food into your body with reasonable portion sizes—just enough to satisfy your hunger.

There will be days when you binge. You might eat four slices of pizza and wash it down with three tall glasses of sugar cola. It's easy to kick yourself and be discouraged. Don't throw in the towel—it's okay. Your body is an amazing machine and can recover quickly. If you fall off your diet, get right back on. A common practice is to use the first day of the week as your *start the diet* day. If you cheat and have three pieces of cake on a Wednesday, you might say to yourself, "I think I'll just take the rest of the week off and start again strong on Monday; I've blown it anyway." This is the wrong approach. If you fall, the time to get up is now, at this very instant. If you cheat and blow your diet, don't despair, just make sure your very next meal follows the 6 rules of successful dieting and you will be right back on track.

CARBOHYDRATE LOADING FOR REDUCED CALORIE DIETS

If you are trying to lose weight using a reduced calorie diet in combination with high intensity training, it is important to make sure that you have adequate energy for workouts. Reduced calorie diets cause your body to burn off a large portion of its stored carbohydrate (glycogen). This depletes energy in your muscles and liver and lessens the potency of workouts. There must be a ready supply of energy in the form of carbohydrates to burn while working out. The best solution to this problem is to prepare for workouts by carbo-loading.

Carbo-loading is done by figuring your daily calorie need and adding 500 calories to that amount in the form of high quality complex and simple carbs like whole grains, rice, legumes, fruits or 100% fruit juices. This technique should be cycled into your workout schedule. If you train 2 to 3 times per week with weights, carbo-load once a week the day before one of your weekly workouts. If you train less then twice a week, carbo-load the day before each workout.

Carbo-loading helps you have the energy to train with enough intensity to maintain and build new muscle mass. If you don't overeat, you will still maintain a calorie deficit on most days. You will more efficiently reach your body-fat loss goals.

Your body needs water to load the muscles and liver with carbohydrates. On carbo-loading days, drink at least 64 ounces (1/2 gallon) of water. If a half-gallon of water is difficult to drink, try fruit juices along with water. Fruit juice contains simple carbohydrates (sugars) as well as fluids and can help load your muscles in one punch. Once you have finished your workout, you may continue your reduced calorie diet plan.

CHAPTER SUMMARY

APPLICATION

DIETING: A STEP-BY-STEP PLAN

- The first step to effective dieting is to calculate the daily caloric need. This is done by executing the following steps:
  - o Calculate the daily caloric need.
  - o Fine-tune the daily caloric need by tracking calories for 1 week.
  - o Add or subtract 500 calories a day to find the daily caloric requirement.
  - o Count calorie intake for another week.
  - o Add or subtract 500 calories a day to gain or lose weight.
- It takes 21 days to break a bad habit and replace it with a good one.
- The 6 rules of healthy dieting are:
  - o Rule 1: Protein and Carbohydrate Balance - a good diet consists of 1-part proteins and 2 parts carbohydrates.
  - o Rule 2: The Half-portion Rule - portion sizes should be kept at a level to satisfy, not to fill.
  - o Rule 3: Watch When You Eat - small meals should be spanned throughout the day. A day should include 3 full meals and no more than 2 snacks, spread equally between meals.
  - o Rule 4: Eat Nutrient-rich Calories - calories should come from nutrient rich foods like whole wheat breads, fruits, vegetables and lean meats like chicken and pork.
  - o Rule 5: Drink Water – drink 64 ounces of water as a minimum every day. Drink a tall glass of water before every meal.
  - o Rule 6: Don't Get Discouraged - after cheating on a diet, it is essential to move on and start dieting again from the moment of the cheat. It is a bad habit to wait for the beginning of the next week to restart a healthy diet.
- Low-carb dieting is not conducive to high intensity training. It is important to load up on carbohydrates the day before a workout to provide adequate energy for training.

MASTER CONCEPT 4: STAYING STRONG

BODY BASICS	→	TRAINING	→	DIETING	**STAYING STRONG**

- Proper weight measurement involves use of a skin-fold caliper along with the bathroom scale.
- Body measurements should be taken using a measuring tape at regular intervals.
- The best way to track progress is by keeping a success journal.
- A success journal should contain goal pages.
- A success journal should contain body measurement pages.

CHAPTER 17: MEASURING YOUR SUCCESS

PRINCIPLES

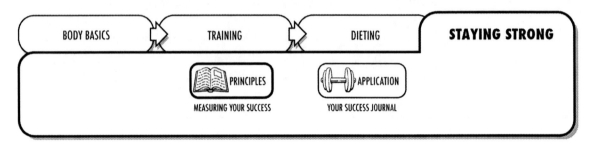

CHAPTER PREVIEW

Seeing success in the form of lost body fat and muscle tone is the best way to stay motivated. The bathroom scale alone isn't an accurate measurement of progress. A skin-fold caliper can be used to figure body fat percentage. Body measurements should be taken on a consistent basis using a measuring tape.

Success Begets Success

What is it that fosters consistent and measurable success? Some seem to be blessed with an amazing ability to succeed at virtually any endeavor in life. Others struggle along, tripping over every bump in the road. If the principles of success could be locked down in a glass display case and explored under just the right conditions, what could we learn?

One principle of success stands true in all classes and in all cases; success begets success. Success is like a single celled organism that divides into 2, then 4, then 8 and so on. Pretty soon there are thousands of single celled organisms populating an area. Like the single celled organism, success reproduces upon itself.

Whether it is finances, relationships, the workplace or any other endeavor you set after, the confidence success brings will motivate you to do more, achieve more and be more.

This concept translates to your weight loss and toning goals. If you can see success in the form of a thinner waist, harder pecs and abs and a younger looking body, you are going to become addicted to the feeling of success. The best way to see success is to carefully track your progress. You must keep records as you lose weight, tone up and get closer to that body you want.

The Art of Effective Goal Setting

Goals should be healthy and reasonable. If you have a goal to lose 10 pounds a week, you probably won't attain it. Unreachable goals will do nothing but discourage you. A goal to lose 2 pounds of body fat each week until reaching a scale weight of 175 pounds is realistic for a five foot ten inch man; this goal is reasonable and attainable.

Once you write a goal, stick to it. Your goal might be to lose 10 pounds of body fat in 5 weeks. In the first 2 weeks, you might lose 4 pounds. Encouraged by your rapid progress, you might be tempted to change your goal to a 15 or 20 pound loss in that same 5 week time period. This is called goal creep. Don't let it happen.

Once your sights are set on a goal, keep them locked in. Keep the same clearly written goal until it is accomplished. You might surpass your written goal; that's great; but don't stretch your goal once it is written. Nothing is more encouraging than reaching a carefully written goal. Nothing is more discouraging than never reaching a goal because it keeps changing and stretching. Once a goal is written, it is written in stone. You don't want to be shooting at a moving target.

After accomplishing a clearly written goal, write down a few notes. Write feelings and insights that you have gained from accomplishing the goal. Put down a few sentences detailing how you feel about yourself after accomplishing the goal. Most importantly, set a new goal. You should always have a written goal to shoot for.

THE SCALE DOESN'T TELL THE WHOLE TRUTH

The quickest and most widely used method of tracking health is stepping onto the old bathroom scale and reading the number. Guess what, the bathroom scale doesn't tell the whole story. How thin are you? How tone are you? How muscular are you? Your bathroom scale doesn't tell you all these things, but you need to know them.

You are an individual. You are different than anyone else. Your physical makeup is different than anyone else's. Let's take a look at a couple of examples; a man and a woman; we'll call them Joe and Jill.

Joe steps onto the bathroom scale and finds that he weighs 180 pounds with a big gut hanging over his waistband and soft pecs, bouncing like Jell-O.

A trained athlete, of the exact same height as Joe, can step on the scale and weigh 185 pounds but have rock-hard abs, pecs and biceps. This is because muscle mass is more dense and heavier than fat mass.

Jill steps onto the scale and discovers that she weighs 150 pounds with flabby arms and is up a few pant sizes from last year, yet her weight has not changed.

A female athlete, in superb condition with low body fat and plenty of calorie burning lean muscle mass, can step onto the same scale and weigh the same 150 pounds, but have gorgeous, defined legs and toned abs.

These comparisons are entirely plausible. Since the scale does not give you the whole picture, it's better to get an overall body status by measuring your body fat percentage along with scale weight to determine your muscle to fat ratio.

What is muscle to fat ratio? Let's go back to our example of flabby Joe vs. the athlete. Joe steps onto the bathroom scale and checks his weight at 180 pounds with a big gut and jell-o pecs. He checks his body fat and finds that he is at a whopping 30% body fat. According to the American Heart Association, Joe qualifies as obese.

The weight trainer, who weighed in at 185 pounds, measures his body fat at 8%. He weighs 5 pounds more than Joe on the bathroom scale but has a lower percentage of body fat because of his high muscle (or lean) weight. Obviously we all want to look like the trained, athletic man or the toned woman with a tight butt and sexy legs.

When following an exercise program, especially one that involves weight lifting, you can expect to gain a few pounds over the first few weeks, even with good hearty workouts and a strict, low calorie diet. This can be discouraging if you don't realize that this is a common beginning response. Lifting weights causes gains in strength, functionality, and lean muscle mass. Your body's composition changes by reducing your percentage of fat and increasing the amount of muscle you carry. Lean muscle mass is three times denser than fat and weighs much more. When you work out with weights you lose fat pounds, but gain muscle weight. Often the rate of weight gain from increased muscle mass is greater than the rate of fat weight loss as the fat comes off. Patience is required until the transition is complete. In the meantime more measurements than mere scale weight are needed to monitor your progress and determine success.

A tool called the skin fold caliper (Figure 17-1) is excellent for tracking your body's muscle to fat ratio.

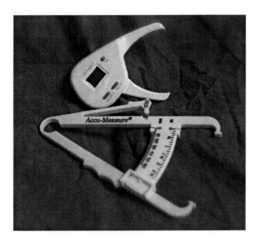

Figure 17-1

With this tool, you can get an accurate measurement of your body's composition by using both a bathroom scale and a skin fold caliper.

NOTE:
You can purchase a full range of body measurement devices from Total Human. Total Human offers various types of skin fold caliper fat measuring devices from simple and inexpensive models to professional, digital devices. For details, visit www.totalhuman.com.

For example, let's say you have a goal to lose 8 pounds in one month. That works out to 2 pounds per week--healthy and reasonable. You write your scale weight and fat percentage readings down. You start with a scale weight of 130 pounds and 21% body fat.

After working hard for a month, you measure again. You find that your scale weight has dropped to 125 pounds; a 5-pound drop is pretty good for one month's work. However, your goal was to drop 2 pounds a week, which would have put you at 122 pounds. You are disappointed. You measure your fat percentage using a skin fold caliper and find that your body fat has dropped 6%. You have gone from 21% to 15% in one month. You do a quick calculation and determine that you have actually lost 8.55 pounds of body fat. You have exceeded your goal by a half a pound. You have also gained 3.55 pounds of valuable lean muscle mass. This works out to be a 12.1-pound change in your body's composition. That is tremendous progress.

Figures 17-2 through 17-5 demonstrate this example.

BEFORE		**AFTER**	
BEGINNING SCALE WEIGHT	130 LBS	ENDING SCALE WEIGHT	125 LBS
BEGINNING FAT PERCENTAGE	21%	ENDING FAT PERCENTAGE	15%
POUNDS OF FAT	27.3	POUNDS OF FAT	18.75
POUNDS OF LEAN MUSCLE MASS	102.7	POUNDS OF LEAN MUSCLE MASS	106.25

Figure 17-2

BEGINNING TOTAL FAT POUNDS	27.3
ENDING TOTAL FAT POUNDS	18.75
TOTAL POUNDS OF FAT	8.55

Figure 17-3

BEGINNING POUNDS OF LEAN MUSCLE MASS	102.7
ENDING POUNDS OF LEAN MUSCLE MASS	106.25
TOTAL POUNDS OF LEAN MUSCLE MASS	3.55

Figure 17-4

TOTAL POUNDS OF FAT LOST	8.55
TOTAL POUNDS OF MUSCLE MASS GAINED	3.55
TOTAL CHANGE IN BODY COMPOSTION	12.1

Figure 17-5

Tracking your success in this manner is the best way to stay motivated. Using the bathroom scale along with the skin fold caliper is the best way to track your success.

CHAPTER SUMMARY

PRINCIPLES

MEASURING YOUR SUCCESS

- Seeing success is the best motivator for continued success.
- Goals are essential to finding success in any endeavor.
- Goals must have a definite set of ambitions and an absolute deadline.
- Once a goal is set, it is important to see it through without changing it along the way.
- The bathroom scale doesn't tell the whole story.
- An accurate assessment of body composition can only be measured by determining scale weight and body fat percentage.
- The skin fold caliper is the quickest and most convenient way to determine fat percentage.

Chapter 18: Your Success Journal

Application

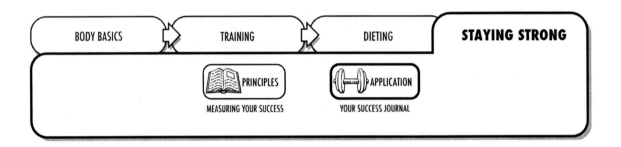

| BODY BASICS | TRAINING | DIETING | STAYING STRONG |

PRINCIPLES
MEASURING YOUR SUCCESS

APPLICATION
YOUR SUCCESS JOURNAL

Chapter Preview

Keeping a success journal is the best way to stay motivated. There should be 3 types of pages in a success journal; goal pages, progress measurement pages and workout record sheets. Goals should be realistic and attainable.

THE SUCCESS JOURNAL

You can stay motivated by keeping a personal success journal with pictures, measurements and notes, detailing your mental status and physical improvements along your training path.

Everything you need to create a motivating success journal can be found in the appendix of this book. Once you have created your success journal, you should value it like the important document it is. You should keep it in a special place. You should review it often. Nothing will motivate you more than a well-kept success journal.

Your success journal should consist of 3 different page types; goal pages, progress measurement pages and workout record sheets. These 3 types of pages together will help you track your progress.

GOAL SHEETS

Every sport has a goal. Football has the touchdown; darts has the bulls-eye; baseball has the homerun. Fitness training is no exception. The beauty of fitness training is that you have the final word on the nature of your goal.

Goal pages in your success journal are an essential part of your success. The first step in your fitness program should be to make a copy of the blank goal page in the appendix of this book and fill it out.

STEP 1: TAKE A PICTURE

Start by taking a picture of yourself. The old cliché says *a picture is worth a thousand words*; there is a lot of wisdom in this adage. A good honest photograph is the only way to see yourself objectively. Don't be afraid to slip into a bathing suit and have your spouse, partner or friend snap away. Remember, this is the before stage. The after photo will look much better.

Paste the photograph onto the first goal page of your journal and write in your name and the date that the photo was taken (Figure 18-1).

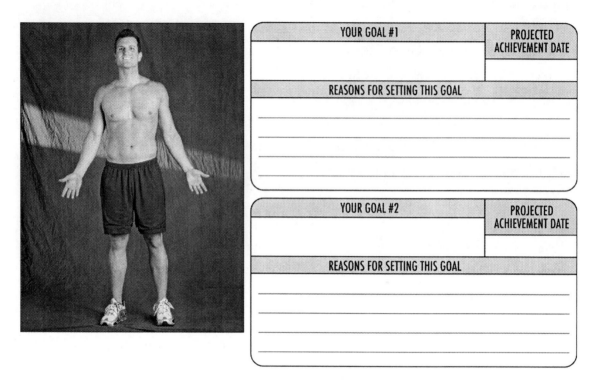

Figure 18-1

STEP 2: WRITE YOUR GOALS

The next step is to write your goals. Blank goal sheets have a mini-form that helps you detail up to 2 goals (Figure 18-2). An effective goal has 3 parts; the goal itself, the deadline by which the goal is meant to be accomplished and the reason(s) why the goal must be achieved. Write the deadline for each of your goals in the provided boxes. Write 1 to 3 reasons why you want to attain each goal; this will act as fuel to help keep you motivated.

TOTALhuman
GOALSHEET

NAME _John Jones_

DATE _Mar 23, 2007_

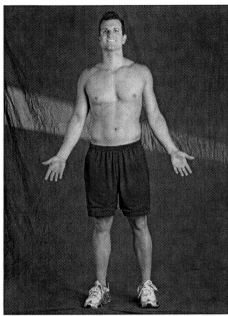

YOUR GOAL #1	PROJECTED ACHIEVEMENT DATE
Lose 10 lbs. of body fat	*5/28/2007*

REASONS FOR SETTING THIS GOAL
Reduce belly fat
Have more energy
Get in the habit of working out

YOUR GOAL #2	PROJECTED ACHIEVEMENT DATE
Bench press 200 lbs.	*5/28/2007*

REASONS FOR SETTING THIS GOAL
Tone my chest
Increase my strength

Figure 18-2

Make sure your goals are realistic. Below are some examples of potential goals:

- Drop your body fat percentage to 15%
- Lose three inches from your belly
- Gain five pounds of lean muscle mass
- Bench press 200 pounds

STEP 3: WRITE YOUR FEELINGS

Your physical strength and muscle development are not the only important things when it comes to fitness training. An effective fitness program brings more to your life than a well-toned body. You will find improvements in every aspect of your life. Your success journal is a place for you to log your success along the road. Write about your relationships, your work, your daily struggles. A goal page is a good place to capture a snapshot of you; both physically and mentally. How are you feeling? Write it on your goal page (Figure 18-3).

HOW DO YOU FEEL?

I have felt tired at work lately. I could use something to get me going in the morning. I think that an exercise program might do the trick. My wife and I have decided to try High Intensity Training from the Total Human book. It sounds good to us. We'll see how it goes.

Figure 18-3

Your success journal is the best tool to help you track your progress. Review your most recent goal page often and compare it to progress made on your workout sheets. As you get closer to attaining your written goals, you will get excited and learn to love high intensity training; there is no motivator like success.

When you hit a goal date, whether or not you have attained your written goal, fill out a new goal page and bind it into your success journal. You should always have at least one clearly defined goal with a deadline and good reasons for why you want to attain that goal.

PROGRESS MEASUREMENT SHEETS AND WORKOUT LOG SHEETS

Along with goals, you must track your progress along the road to health. This is done in two ways. Each time you workout and fill out a workout sheet, make sure you bind it into your success journal. These workout sheets will become an invaluable tool to help you increase or decrease your working weight and to calculate rest and recovery days between workouts.

The second way to track your progress is by using *progress measurement sheets*. Blanks of these sheets can be found in the appendix of this book. Feel free to copy and use them as often as you like.

Progress measurement sheets contain essential measurements of your body that will help you track your strength gain, weight loss and fat percentage loss. Your first progress measurement page should be at the front of your journal, just behind your first goal page. On this page, you should write the beginning date of your training program. Progress measurement sheets should be filled out using the following steps:

STEP 1: TAKE A PICTURE

The progress measurement page is the most effective way for you to track your body's development throughout your training regimen. The best way to see results is to take a picture of yourself. By taking a picture, you will have the ability to objectively view your body and diagnose where you need the most work. Don't feel self conscious about taking a picture; this is perhaps one of the most important parts of your overall training evaluation.

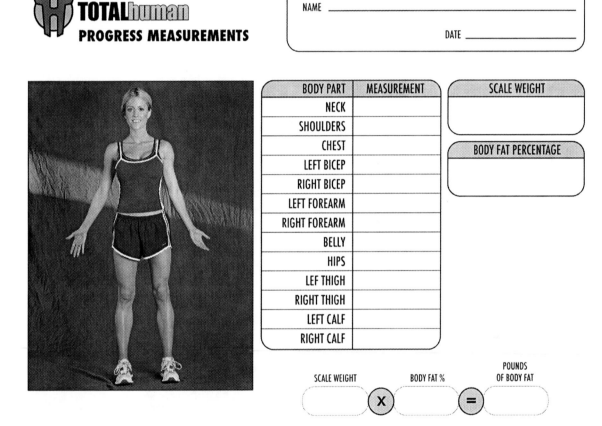

TOTALhuman **PROGRESS MEASUREMENTS**

NAME _____

DATE _____

BODY PART	MEASUREMENT
NECK	
SHOULDERS	
CHEST	
LEFT BICEP	
RIGHT BICEP	
LEFT FOREARM	
RIGHT FOREARM	
BELLY	
HIPS	
LEF THIGH	
RIGHT THIGH	
LEFT CALF	
RIGHT CALF	

SCALE WEIGHT

BODY FAT PERCENTAGE

SCALE WEIGHT ⓧ BODY FAT % ⟳ POUNDS OF BODY FAT

Figure 18-4

STEP 2: TAKE MEASUREMENTS

It is essential to keep track of your basic measurements in inches over your entire body. Measurements should be taken at regular intervals throughout training (perhaps every 10 workouts). Use a measuring tape and follow the tutorials found in Figure 18-5 and Figure 18-6. Write your measurements on a progress measurement page next to a photograph of yourself.

BODY MEASUREMENTS

NECK

Wrap a measuring tape just below the Adams apple for men or midway between the chin and the shoulders for women.

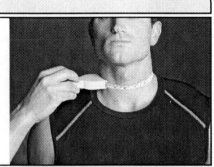

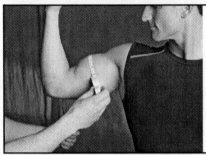

UPPER ARM

Wrap a measuring tape in a straight line around the largest area of the upper arm. Hold the arm parallel to the floor and flex while taking the measurement.

FOREARM

Extend the elbow completely. Make a fist to flex the forearm. Wrap a measuring tape in a straight line around the largest part of the forearm.

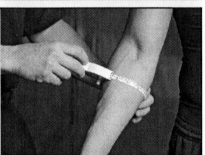

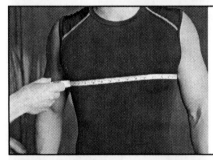

CHEST

With the shoulders squared, stand upright and measure around the torso with the tape running in a horizontal line over the nipples.

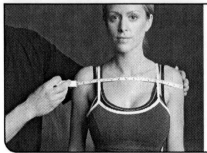

SHOULDERS

With the shoulders squared, stand upright and measure around the shoulders with the tape running in a horizontal line around the largest part of the shoulder area.

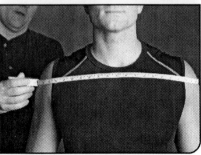

Figure 18-5

BODY MEASUREMENTS (CONTINUED)

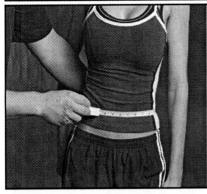
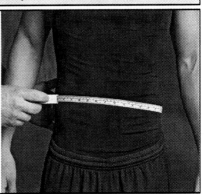

WAIST

Wrap a measuring tape in a horizontal line around the waist at the level of the navel.

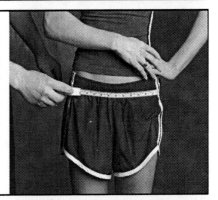

HIPS

Stand straight up with the heels together and with your weight evenly distributed on both feet. Wrap a measuring tape in a horizontal line around the hips at the largest point of the glutes.

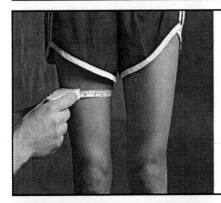
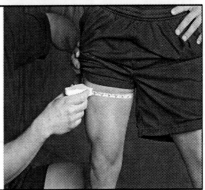

THIGHS

Stand straight up with the feet at a shoulder width stance. Evenly distribute your weight on your feet. Wrap a measuring tape around the upper thigh, just below the glutes. Do not flex the thigh muscles while measuring.

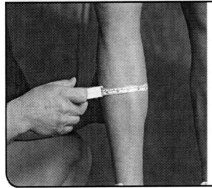
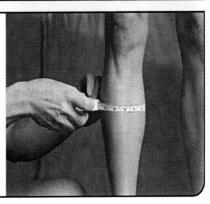

CALVES

Stand straight up with the feet at a shoulder width stance. Evenly distribute your weight on your feet. Wrap a measuring tape around the largest part of the calf muscle. Do not flex the calf muscle while measuring.

Figure 18-6

After pasting a photograph of yourself onto a blank progress measurement page and writing in your measurements, your progress measurement page should look like Figure 18-7.

PROGRESS MEASUREMENTS

NAME _Jane Smith_

DATE _Mar 23, 2007_

BODY PART	MEASUREMENT
NECK	12.5
SHOULDERS	36.25
CHEST	34.5
LEFT BICEP	10.0
RIGHT BICEP	10.0
LEFT FOREARM	8.25
RIGHT FOREARM	8.25
BELLY	26.75
HIPS	33.0
LEF THIGH	18.5
RIGHT THIGH	18.5
LEFT CALF	15.0
RIGHT CALF	15.0

SCALE WEIGHT

BODY FAT PERCENTAGE

SCALE WEIGHT		BODY FAT %		POUNDS OF BODY FAT
	X		=	

Figure 18-7

STEP 3: RECORD SCALE WEIGHT AND BODY FAT PERCENTAGE

To get an accurate evaluation of your body's fat percentage, you must take both your bathroom scale weight and your fat percentage measurements.

There are many ways to get your body fat percentage. The most accurate is weighing the body while under water, but that option involves the use of expensive equipment and is not always accessible. Another way is to purchase a bathroom scale with an infrared sensor to read your body fat percentage; but infrared measurement is usually inaccurate. Some bathroom scales request information like your age, sex, height and weight. These criteria are used to perform a simple calculation to determine your body fat percentage. This formulated approach does not take pounds of muscle mass into consideration and is usually flawed.

The most accessible and reliable way to read your body fat percentage is to use a skin fold caliper.

The skin fold caliper is simple to use. Skin fold caliper measurements should be taken at three places on the right side of your body. The three measurement areas are different for men (Figure 18-8) and women (Figure 18-9).

SKIN FOLD CALIPER MEASUREMENT FOR MEN

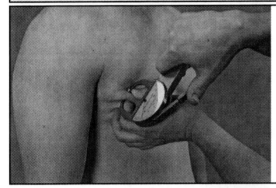

FIRST MEASUREMENT

The first measurement is taken by relaxing the muscles of the chest, pinching the skin on the right side of the chest and using the caliper to get a reading.

SECOND MEASUREMENT

The second measurement is taken by relaxing the muscles of the stomach, pinching the skin of the umbilicus or the right bottom side of the belly and using the caliper to get a reading.

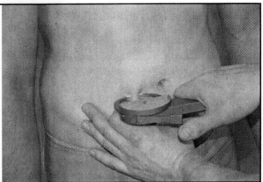

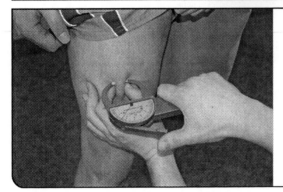

THIRD MEASUREMENT

The third measurement is taken by relaxing the muscles in the legs, pinching the skin on the outside of the mid, right thigh and using the skin fold caliper to get a reading.

Figure 18-8

SKIN FOLD CALIPER MEASUREMENT FOR WOMEN

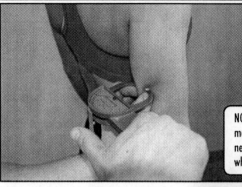

FIRST MEASUREMENT

The first measurement is taken by relaxing the muscles in the arms and having a friend pinch the back of the mid, right triceps and taking a reading.

NOTE: getting an accurate mid-triceps skin fold measurement is impossible to do by yourself. You will need the help of a friend so you can remain relaxed while the measurement is being taken.

SECOND MEASUREMENT

The second measurement is taken by relaxing the muscles around the waist and pinching a diagonal fold at a 45-degree angle just above the hip bone and getting a reading with the skin fold calipers.

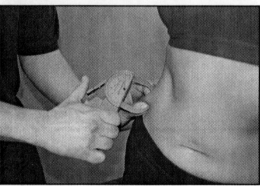

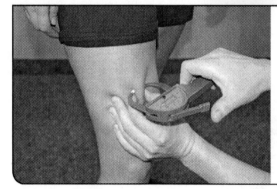

THIRD MEASUREMENT

The third measurement is taken by relaxing the muscles of the legs, pinching the skin on the outer, right mid-thigh and getting a measurement with the skin fold calipers.

Figure 18-9

Once these measurements have been taken, you can accurately determine your body fat percentage by referencing Figure 18-10 for men and Figure 18-11 for women. By adding the 3 skin fold measurements in millimeters together and cross-referencing the sum against your age category on the table for your sex, you will find your body's fat percentage.

PERCENT FAT ESTIMATE FOR MEN:
SUM OF CHEST, ABDOMEN AND THIGH SKINFOLD MEASUREMENTS

SUM OF SKINFOLDS (mm)	CURRENT AGE								
	UNDER 22	23 - 27	28 - 32	33 - 37	38 - 42	43 - 47	48 - 52	53 - 57	OVER 57
8-10	1.3	1.8	2.3	2.9	3.4	3.9	4.5	5	5.5
11-13	2.2	2.8	3.3	3.9	4.4	4.9	5.5	6	6.5
14-16	3.2	3.8	4.3	4.8	5.4	5.9	6.4	7	7.5
17-19	4.2	4.7	5.3	5.8	6.3	6.9	7.4	8	8.5
20-22	5.1	5.7	6.2	6.8	7.3	7.9	8.4	8.9	9.5
23-25	6.1	6.6	7.2	7.7	8.3	8.8	9.4	9.9	10.5
26-28	7	7.6	8.1	8.7	9.2	9.8	10.3	10.9	11.4
29-31	8	8.5	9.1	9.6	10.2	10.7	11.3	11.8	12.4
32-34	8.9	9.4	10	10.5	11.1	11.6	12.2	12.8	13.3
35-37	9.8	10.4	10.9	11.5	12	12.6	13.1	13.7	14.3
38-40	10.7	11.3	11.8	12.4	12.9	13.5	14.1	14.6	15.2
41-43	11.6	12.2	12.7	13.3	13.8	14.4	15	15.5	16.1
44-46	12.5	13.1	13.6	14.2	14.7	15.3	15.9	16.4	17
47-49	13.4	13.9	14.5	15.1	15.6	16.2	16.8	17.3	17.9
50-52	14.3	14.8	15.4	15.9	16.5	17.1	17.6	18.2	18.8
53-55	15.1	15.7	16.2	16.8	17.4	17.9	18.5	19.1	19.7
56-58	16	16.5	17.1	17.7	18.2	18.8	19.4	20	20.5
59-61	16.9	17.4	17.9	18.5	19.1	19.7	20.2	20.8	21.4
62-64	17.6	18.2	18.8	19.4	19.9	20.5	21.1	21.7	22.2
65-67	18.5	19	19.6	20.2	20.8	21.3	21.9	22.5	23.1
68-70	19.3	19.9	20.4	21	21.6	22.2	22.7	23.3	23.9
71-73	20.1	20.7	21.2	21.8	22.4	23	23.6	24.1	24.7
74-76	20.9	21.5	22	22.6	23.2	23.8	24.4	25	25.5
77-79	21.7	22.2	22.8	23.4	24	24.6	25.2	25.8	26.3
80-82	22.4	23	23.6	24.2	24.8	25.4	25.9	26.5	27.1
83-85	23.2	23.8	24.4	25	25.5	26.1	26.7	27.3	27.9
86-88	24	24.5	25.1	25.7	26.3	26.9	27.5	28.1	28.7
89-91	24.7	25.3	25.9	26.5	27.1	27.6	28.2	28.8	29.4
92-94	25.4	26	26.6	27.2	27.8	28.4	29	29.6	30.2
95-97	26.1	26.7	27.3	27.9	28.5	29.1	29.7	30.3	30.9
98-100	26.9	27.4	28	28.6	29.2	29.8	30.4	31	31.6
101-103	27.5	28.1	28.7	29.3	29.9	30.5	31.1	31.7	32.3
104-106	28.2	28.8	29.4	30	30.6	31.2	31.8	32.4	33
107-109	28.9	29.5	30.1	30.7	31.3	31.9	32.5	33.1	33.7
110-112	29.6	30.2	30.8	31.4	32	32.6	33.2	33.8	34.4
113-115	30.2	30.8	31.4	32	32.6	33.2	33.8	34.5	35.1
116-118	30.9	31.5	32.1	32.7	33.3	33.9	34.5	35.1	35.7
119-121	31.5	32.1	32.7	33.3	33.9	34.5	35.1	35.7	36.4
122-124	32.1	32.7	33.3	33.9	34.5	35.1	35.8	36.4	37
125-127	32.7	33.3	33.9	34.5	35.1	35.8	36.4	37	37.6

Figure 18-10

PERCENT FAT ESTIMATE FOR WOMEN:
SUM OF CHEST, ABDOMEN AND THIGH SKINFOLD MEASUREMENTS

SUM OF SKINFOLDS (mm)	CURRENT AGE								
	UNDER 22	23 - 27	28 - 32	33 - 37	38 - 42	43 - 47	48 - 52	53 - 57	OVER 57
23-25	9.7	9.9	10.2	10.4	10.7	10.9	11.2	11.4	11.7
26-28	11	11.2	11.5	11.7	12	12.3	12.5	12.7	13
29-31	12.3	12.5	12.8	13	13.3	13.5	13.8	14	14.3
32-34	13.6	13.8	14	14.3	14.5	14.8	15	15.3	15.5
35-37	14.8	15	15.3	15.5	15.8	16	16.3	16.52	16.8
38-40	16	16.3	16.5	16.7	17	17.2	17.5	17.7	18
41-43	17.2	17.4	17.7	17.9	18.2	18.4	18.7	18.9	19.2
44-46	18.3	18.6	18.8	19.1	19.3	19.6	19.8	20.1	20.3
47-49	19.5	19.7	20	20.2	20.5	20.7	21	21.2	21.5
50-52	20.6	20.8	21.1	21.3	21.6	21.8	22.1	22.3	22.6
53-55	21.7	21.9	22.1	22.4	22.6	22.9	23.1	23.4	23.6
56-58	22.7	23	23.2	23.4	23.7	23.9	24.2	24.4	24.7
59-61	23.7	24	24.2	24.5	24.7	25	25.2	25.5	25.7
62-64	24.7	25	25.2	25.5	25.7	26	26.2	26.4	26.7
65-67	25.7	25.9	26.2	26.4	26.7	26.9	27.2	27.4	27.7
68-70	26.6	26.9	27.1	27.4	27.6	27.9	28.1	28.4	28.6
71-73	27.5	27.8	28	28.3	28.5	28.8	29	29.3	29.5
74-76	28.4	28.7	28.9	29.2	29.4	29.7	29.9	30.2	30.4
77-79	29.3	29.5	29.8	30	30.3	30.5	30.8	31	31.3
80-82	30.1	30.4	30.6	30.9	31.1	31.4	31.6	31.9	32.1
83-85	30.9	31.2	31.4	31.7	31.9	32.2	32.4	32.7	32.9
86-88	31.7	32	32.2	32.5	32.7	32.9	33.2	33.4	33.7
89-91	32.5	32.7	33	33.2	33.5	33.7	33.9	34.2	34.4
92-94	33.2	33.4	33.7	33.9	34.2	34.4	34.7	34.9	35.2
95-97	33.9	34.1	34.4	34.6	34.9	35.1	35.4	35.6	35.9
98-100	34.6	34.8	35.1	35.3	35.5	35.8	36	36.3	36.5
101-103	35.3	35.4	35.7	35.9	36.2	36.4	36.7	36.9	37.2
104-106	35.8	36.1	36.3	36.6	36.8	37.1	37.3	37.5	37.8
107-109	36.4	36.7	36.9	37.1	37.4	37.6	37.9	38.1	38.4
110-112	37	37.2	37.5	37.7	38	38.2	38.5	38.7	38.9
113-115	37.5	37.8	38	38.2	38.5	38.7	39	39.2	39.5
116-118	38	38.3	38.5	38.8	39	39.3	39.5	39.7	40
119-121	38.5	38.7	39	39.2	39.5	39.7	40	40.2	40.5
122-124	39	39.2	39.4	39.7	39.9	40.2	40.4	40.7	40.9
125-127	39.4	39.6	39.9	40.1	40.4	40.6	40.9	41.1	41.4
128-130	39.8	40	40.3	40.5	40.8	41	41.3	41.5	41.8

Figure 18-11

After getting your scale weight and body fat percentage, write these two numbers onto your progress measurement page in the provided boxes (Figure 18-12).

TOTALhuman
PROGRESS MEASUREMENTS

NAME _Jane Smith_

DATE _Mar 23, 2007_

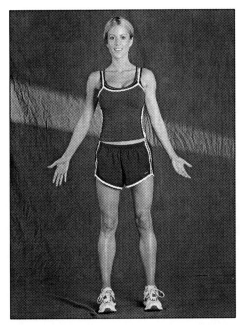

BODY PART	MEASUREMENT
NECK	12.5
SHOULDERS	36.25
CHEST	34.5
LEFT BICEP	10.0
RIGHT BICEP	10.0
LEFT FOREARM	8.25
RIGHT FOREARM	8.25
BELLY	26.75
HIPS	33.0
LEF THIGH	18.5
RIGHT THIGH	18.5
LEFT CALF	15.0
RIGHT CALF	15.0

SCALE WEIGHT
129 lbs.

BODY FAT PERCENTAGE
12%

SCALE WEIGHT ( ) **X** BODY FAT % ( ) **=** POUNDS OF BODY FAT ( )

Figure 18-12

A simple calculation is provided on the progress measurement sheet to help you determine how many pounds of your body are fat and how many pounds are muscle. Write in your scale weight and body fat % divided by 100 between the provided boxes (Figure 18-13). Multiply the scale weight by the decimal value in the body fat % brackets and you will get the number of fat pounds in your body.

SCALE WEIGHT **220** **X** BODY FAT % **.40** **=** POUNDS OF BODY FAT **88 lbs.**

Figure 18-13

As your body changes and improves, the number of fat pounds is much more important than your scale weight in determining your progress. It is entirely feasible for your scale weight to go up, but your fat pounds to go down during a high intensity training regimen. If this happens, congratulations, you are on the right track.

STEP 4: WRITE YOUR FEELINGS

After pasting a picture and noting your measurements on a blank progress measurement sheet, it's time to step back and evaluate your progress. Take a look at the photograph of yourself and read through the measurements. If there are earlier progress measurement sheets bound into your success journal, evaluate those as well. Look at your progress and ask yourself a few questions. Are you on track to make your goal? Are you ahead of schedule? Are you behind schedule? If you are behind schedule, was your goal unrealistic? Have you lapsed in your high intensity training regimen?

After evaluating your progress, write your thoughts in the provided area at the bottom of the sheet. This is a good opportunity for you to note your mental status as well as your physical status. Write about your performance in other areas of your life. Write about your relationships, your job—anything you want.

With progress measurement sheets, goal sheets and workout sheets, your journal will become a tremendously detailed log of your health and training. Your success journal will become your best friend. It will motivate you like no other tool. To start on any training regimen without a success journal is a mistake. Keep it current and keep it accurate.

NOTE:

Total Human offers another excellent product to help you stay on track. *The Workout Training Journal* **is a power-packed high intensity program and training journal all-in-one.** *The Workout Training Journal* **is a training boot camp that takes you through 30 high intensity weight-training workouts.** *The Workout Training Journal* **is a handsomely bound journal. It includes goal and measurement pages at the beginning and progress measurement pages after every 10 workouts to help you track your development along the way.** *The Workout Training Journal* **takes about 12 weeks to complete and promises astounding results. For more information, go to www.totalhuman.com.**

CHAPTER SUMMARY

APPLICATION

YOUR SUCCESS JOURNAL

- The success journal is an essential part of any exercise regimen.
- The success journal contains goal pages.
- Goal pages should be placed at the beginning of the success journal and after the completion of goals written on earlier goal pages.
- Goal pages should contain the following elements:
    - o   A photograph
    - o   Goals with forecasted completion dates and descriptions
    - o   Thoughts and feelings
- The Success journal contains progress measurement pages.
- Progress measurement pages should be written and placed into the success journal at regular intervals (once a month or every 2 weeks).
- Progress measurement pages should contain the following elements:
    - o   A photograph
    - o   Tape measurements of essential body parts
    - o   Scale weight and body fat percentage
    - o   Thoughts and feelings
- Individual workout sheets should be placed in the success journal chronologically as workouts are performed.

CHAPTER 19: IT'S ALL UP TO YOU

Close your eyes for a moment and imagine that perfect body you have always wanted.

Men, imagine perfect pecs, biceps, and razor defined triceps. Imagine walking into a room chest first. Imagine a six-pack and less than 10% body fat.

Women, imagine shapely legs, arms and shoulders. Imagine watching every head turn as you walk by. Imagine your friends noticing you as if they are seeing you for the first time-- saying things like "you look younger" or "you've lost a lot of weight; you look great."

With the life-changing principles you have learned from this book you can have that perfect body. You can improve every facet of your life. Expect more energy. Expect more mental focus and a better memory. Expect a desire to do those things you have procrastinated in the past. Expect a better marriage or relationship with your partner. Good health is the foundation of all things wonderful in life. You will live better. You will have a fuller, richer life. You will develop the ability to conquer any obstacle in your path.

You have the knowledge; you have the tools. You have learned your body's natural language. Now it's up to you. So what are you waiting for? Get going! And good luck on your newfound road to good health and success.

APPENDIX A: GLOSSARY

Abdominals - The muscles of the belly.

Abdominals Muscle Group - See abdominals.

Activity Level - The amount of daily activity one performs such as exercise, walking, running and working.

Adaptation – A process the muscles go through after a specific high intensity activity to improve themselves in order to better handle the task in the future.

Adrenaline - A hormone that is secreted into the blood stream as the result of physical or mental stress. It stimulates heart action. It also increases blood pressure, metabolic rate and blood glucose concentration.

Aerobic - With oxygen.

Aerobic Energy System - The energy system of the body that uses oxygen and fat as fuels to perform mid to low intensity activities like jogging or biking.

Aerobic Training - Repeated exercise of the aerobic energy system to force growth and adaptation.

Amino Acids - The building blocks of proteins. There are 20 amino acids in all. Each is a chain of different molecules linked together to form a type of protein.

Anaerobic - Without oxygen.

Anaerobic Energy System - The energy system of the body that does not use oxygen as a resource for energy. The anaerobic energy system is divided into two subsystems; the ATP-Pc system and the Glycolytic energy subsystems. The anaerobic energy system is used for short duration, high intensity activities like lifting heavy weights or sprinting.

Anaerobic Training - Repeated exercise of the anaerobic energy system to force growth and adaptation.

Arrhythmia - An irregularity in the force or rhythm of the heartbeat.

ATP - An element found in the muscles that contains high-energy phosphate bonds. It is used to transport energy to cells for muscle contraction.

ATP-Pc Energy System - The first subsystem in the anaerobic energy system. The ATP-Pc system spends a ready supply of ATP in the muscles and expends its entire supply of energy in the first 10 seconds of high intensity activity like lifting heavy weights or sprinting.

Barbell - A long, heavy bar with weights attached to each end.

Barbell Bench Press - A weight training exercise in which a barbell is lifted repeatedly from the chest to a fully, extended arm position.

Barbell Compound Row - A weight training exercise in which, while standing, a barbell is held in both hands with the arms fully extended downward. The barbell is lifted to the belly button and slowly lowered again. The grip can be either over or underhand. This exercise is meant to strengthen the muscles of the upper back and arms.

Barbell Curl - A weight training exercise in which a barbell is held with both hands, palms up. The weight is moved by bending and straightening the elbows. This exercise is meant to strengthen the bicep muscles.

Barbell Deadlift - A strength training exercise in which the weight is lifted from knee height in a power cage to the level of the hips and then lowered back to the power cage safety bars when finished. This exercise is meant to strengthen the muscles of the lower and upper back, as well as the muscles along the back side of the hips and legs.

Barbell Overhead Press - A strength training exercise in which a barbell is pushed up above the head and lowered to just above the top of the head. This exercise is meant to strengthen the deltoid muscles.

Barbell Preacher Curl - A strength training exercise in which a barbell is held in both hands, palms up and the elbows are bent with the upper arms resting on a slanted bench. This exercise is meant to strengthen the bicep muscles.

Barbell Squat - A strength training exercise in which a barbell is held across the back of the shoulders and the knees are bent to a 90-degree angle, bringing the body to a squatting position. The knees are then straightened to bring the body back to a standing position. This exercise is meant to strengthen the muscles of the upper legs.

Basal Metabolic Rate - The rate at which the body burns calories at rest.

Dumbbell Bent Row - A strength training exercise in which a dumbbell is pulled up with one hand while kneeling over the side of a long bench. This exercise is meant to strengthen the muscles on the and arms.

Biceps - The muscles of the front of the upper arm.

Body Fat Percentage - The percentage of the body that is made up of fat.

Cadence - The time it takes to perform one repetition of any strength training exercise.

Calories - Units of energy. 1 calorie contains enough energy to heat 1 gram of water 1 degree Celsius or 1.8 degrees Fahrenheit.

Calves - The muscles on the back lower legs.

Carbohydrates - Any organic compound that contains sugars, starches, celluloses and gums. Carbohydrates are the major source of energy for humans and animals.

Cardiac Muscle - The muscular tissue of the heart.

Cardiovascular System - See aerobic system.

Chest Muscle Group - The muscles located on the front upper area of the torso.

Complete Proteins - Proteins that contain all 20 amino acids. Complete proteins are typically found in products of animal origin.

Complex Carbohydrates - Carbohydrates that have to be broken down by digestive enzymes before sugars can be absorbed through the intestinal lining.

Compound Exercise – A weight training exercise that recruits the involvement of 2 or more joints.

Congestive Heart Failure - A condition marked by weakness, edema and shortness of breath that is caused by the inability of the heart to maintain adequate blood circulation in the peripheral tissues and lungs.

Contract - To reduce in size by drawing together.

Cool-down - A 5 to 10 minute period of medium to low intensity exercise at the end of a workout.

Deadlift - A strength training exercise in which the weight is lifted from knee height in a power cage to the level of the hips and then lowered back to the power cage safety bars when finished. This exercise is meant to strengthen the muscles of the lower and upper back, as well as the muscles located along the back of the hips and legs.

Decline Bench Press - A strength training exercise in which the weight is pushed from the chest to a fully extended arm position and brought back to the chest again while laying on a decline bench with the head lower than the hips.

Deltoids - The muscles covering the shoulder joint, used to raise the arms from the sides.

Diabetes - Any of several metabolic disorders marked by excessive discharge of urine and persistent thirst.

Diet - The usual food and drink of a person or animal.

Dumbbell - A short bar with weight on both ends used as a tool for strength training exercises.

Dumbbell Curl - A weight training exercise in which dumbbells are held in both hands, palms up. The weight is moved by bending and straightening the elbows. An exercise meant to strengthen the bicep muscles.

Duration - The total amount of time spent working out from the first exercise to the last and every activity in between.

Energy Expenditure - The amount of energy spent in a period of time.

Enzyme - Any of several complex proteins that are produced by cells and act as catalysts in specific biochemical reactions.

Erector Spinae - The muscles of the lower back around the spine.

Exercise - The act of forcing muscles to perform beyond their usual level of activity in order to force growth and adaptation.

Explosive Lifting - Uncontrolled, fast motion while performing exercise with heavy weights.

Fast Twitch Muscle Fibers - Muscle fibers best suited for high intensity, short duration activities like sprinting or lifting heavy weights, characterized by high force and low endurance activities.

Fat - Any of various soft, solid or semisolid organic compounds constituting the esters of glycerol and fatty acids and their associated organic groups.

Fatty Acid - Any of a large group of organic acids derived from fats. Fatty acids are an essential part of supporting the cardiovascular, reproductive, immune and nervous systems.

Flat Bench Press - A strength training exercise in which the weight is pushed from the chest to a fully extended arm position and brought back to the chest again while laying on a flat, level bench. An exercise meant to strengthen the muscles of the chest.

Flexibility training - The act of performing exercises to stretch the muscles, tendons and ligaments of the body in order to increase body flexibility.

Forks - Supports on a bench press where a heavy barbell may be placed.

Form - The biomechanical movement while performing a strength training exercise.

Frequency - How often a person works out.

Glucose - The principle circulating sugar in the blood stream and the major source of energy for the body.

Gluteus - The muscles on the back of the body between the lower back and the upper legs.

Glycogen - The main carbohydrate storage in the body. It occurs primarily in the liver and muscle tissue. Glycogen is readily converted to glucose as needed by the body to satisfy its energy needs.

Glycolitic Energy System - The metabolic breakdown of glucose and other sugars that releases energy in the form of ATP.

Hams - See hamstrings.

Hamstrings - The muscles of the upper back legs.

Heart Attack - A sudden interruption or insufficiency of the supply of blood to the heart, typically resulting from occlusion or obstruction of a coronary artery and often characterized by severe chest pain.

Helper Muscles - Smaller muscles that take a secondary part of lifting. They are said to help major muscles with their assigned tasks.

High Blood Pressure - Abnormally high arterial blood pressure, sometimes accompanied by nervousness, dizziness or headache, also known as hypertension.

High Cholesterol - An abnormally high amount of a white crystalline substance found in tissues and various foods.

High Impact Aerobic Exercise - Any aerobic exercise that involves high and sudden force to the joints tendons and ligaments like running.

High Intensity Training (HIT) – The act of training the anaerobic energy system with a mode of exercise that, due to its intensity, can only be maintained for short bursts of time.

HIT - See high intensity training.

Hormones - A substance produced by one tissue and conveyed by the bloodstream to another to effect physiological activity such as growth or metabolism.

Hypertension - See high blood pressure.

Impact Force - The meeting of downward motion with upward motion to create a high level of force.

Incline Bench Press - A strength training exercise in which the weight is pushed from the chest to a fully extended arm position and brought back to the chest again while laying on an incline bench with the head higher than the hips. An exercise meant to strengthen the muscles of the chest.

Incomplete Proteins – Any of a variety of proteins that lacks one or more of 20 different types of amino acids.

Inroading – The act of, with exercise, rendering the muscles to a temporary state of limited functionality. The main symptoms of inroaded muscles are soreness and stiffness in the muscles following a period of high intensity activity.

Insulin - A hormone that acts as a regulator of the metabolism of carbohydrates and fats, especially the conversion of glucose to glycogen, which lowers the blood glucose level.

Intensity - The level of muscular work performed in a certain time period.

Involuntary Action - An action performed in the body without conscious thought of the action taking place.

Lactic Acid - A by-product in the creation of ATP by the glycolytic energy system thought to be the cause of muscle burn while performing high intensity exercise. It is also thought of as a limiting factor in muscle fibers' ability to contract.

Lats - The muscles of the outer back.

Lean Muscle Mass - A dense mass of muscle containing little fat.

Leg Curl – A strength training exercise in which weight is moved by bending and straightening the knees. Resistance is added to the act of bending the knees. This exercise is meant to strengthen the hamstring muscles.

Leg Extension – A strength training exercise in which weight is moved by bending and straightening the knees. Resistance is added to the act of straightening the knees. This exercise is meant to strengthen the muscles of the quadriceps.

Ligament - A sheet or band of tough tissue connecting bones or cartilage to joints.

Low Impact Aerobic Exercise - Aerobic exercise that does not expose the joints, tendons and ligaments to high impact forces; i.e. bicycling.

Lower Back Muscle Group - The muscles of the lower back, including the erector spinae around the spine.

Lower Legs Muscle Group - The muscles of the lower legs including the calves and tibalis anterior.

Lower Trapezius - The muscles in the upper back found between the shoulder blades.

Lumbar - Of, near or situated in the part of the back and sides between the lowest ribs and the pelvis.

Macro Nutrients – Nutrients such as proteins, fats and carbohydrates.

Maximum Heart Rate (MHR) - A target high-end heart rate when using cardiovascular exercise.

Medium Twitch - Muscle fibers best suited for mid-intensity activities like jogging or heavy yard work.

Metabolic After-burn - The act of the metabolic system to burn calories as a part of growth and adaptation for hours to days after high intensity activity.

Metabolism - The chemical processes occurring within a living cell or organism that are necessary for the maintenance of life. In metabolism some substances are broken down to yield energy for vital processes while other substances, necessary for life, are synthesized.

MHR - See maximum heart rate.

Micro Nutrients – Nutrients such as vitamins, minerals and trace elements.

Military Press - See overhead press.

Muscle Failure - The point during high intensity activity where muscles are forced to cease from activity and take a rest.

Muscle Fibers - Long bundles of tissue that have the ability to contract. When combined, muscle fibers make up muscles, the moving mechanisms of the body.

Muscle group - A collection of muscles in an area of the body such as the upper back muscle group.

Nutrition – The macro and micro nutrients that make up food.

Obesity – An excessive amount of fat mass on the body.

Obliques - The muscles of the lower torso found below the lowest ribs and above the pelvis on the outsides of the torso.

Obliques Muscle Group - See obliques.

Overhead Press – A strength training exercise in which weight is moved by pushing it upward to a fully extended arm position above the head and bringing it down to just above the head. An exercise meant to strengthen the muscles of the deltoids, upper trapezius and triceps.

Oxidative - The use of oxygen to produce energy.

Pancreas - A long, irregularly shaped gland, lying behind the stomach that secretes insulin, glycogen and somatostatin into the blood stream.

Pecs - See pectoralis.

Pectoralis - The muscles of the upper front torso that act to bring the arms across and down the torso.

Peripheral Artery Disease - A condition that impairs blood flow in the arteries due to narrow or blocked arteries. The most common cause of narrow or blocked arteries is fatty deposits.

Power Cage – A device used to perform barbell exercises with heavy weights in which one stands or lays on one's back below safety bars, mounted to a larger structure. These safety bars are meant to hold heavy barbells when one experiences muscle failure during exercise.

Principle of Orderly Recruitment - The order in which muscle fibers are utilized to perform a task. Slow twitch muscle fibers are called first, medium twitch second and fast twitch third. Mid and fast twitch muscle fibers are only called on if the intensity of a task is high enough to require them.

Protein - The fundamental component of all living cells made up of amino acids. Proteins are included in many substances, such as enzymes, hormones and antibodies, that are necessary for the proper functioning of an organism. They are necessary to the growth and repair of tissue and can be obtained from foods such as meat, fish, eggs, milk and legumes.

Pull-downs – A strength training exercise in which weight is moved by pulling it from a full arm extended position above the head to the chest and back to a full arm extended position. An exercise meant to strengthen the muscles of the upper back and biceps.

Purposeful Movement - Slow and even movement while performing a strength training exercise.

Quads - See Quadriceps

Quadriceps - The muscles of the front, upper legs.

Rear Deltoids - The muscles on the back of the shoulders.

Regimen - A consistent, regulated system, such as dieting and/or exercise.

Rep - See repetition.

Repetition - The act of performing one complete exercise such as one bench press.

Resistance - A force that opposes or retards an action, such as adding weight to a dumbbell before lifting it.

Resistance Training - The act of training the muscles by exercising them with weight training exercises to force growth and adaptation.

Rest and Recovery - The period of time between workouts in which inroaded muscles are allowed to rest, grow and adapt.

Rhomboids - The muscles located on both sides of the spine, outside the lower trapezius.

Serratus - The muscles on the front and sides of the torso, just below the armpits.

Set - A group of repetitions, consisting of the same type of strength training exercise performed without interruption.

Shoulder Girdle - The area of the body around the shoulders including the left and right clavicles and the left and right scapula.

Shoulder Shrug - An exercise in which weight is moved by shrugging the shoulders while holding a barbell or dumbbells at a downward, full arm extended position. An exercise meant to strengthen the muscles of the trapezius.

Shoulders Muscle Group - The muscles located in the shoulders, including the deltoids and rear deltoids.

Simple Carbohydrates - Carbohydrates that can be digested quickly, often containing refined sugar and few essential vitamins or minerals.

Single-joint Exercise - Any exercise that involves the bending of only one joint, like dumbbell curls and leg curls.

Skeletal Muscle - Usually voluntary muscle made up of elongated fibers, principally attached to tendons that attach to the bones.

Skin Fold Caliper - A mechanical device with 2 calipers used to measure the percentage of body fat.

Slow Twitch Muscle Fibers - Muscle fibers best suited for low intensity activities like walking, picking up a room or washing dishes.

Smooth Muscle - Muscle tissue that contracts without conscious control, found in the walls of the internal organs, such as the stomach, intestines, bladder and blood vessels.

Spotter - One who is responsible for guarding an individual from injury during the act of lifting heavy weights as a part of exercise.

Squats - An exercise that involves holding dumbbells or a barbell and, from a standing position, bending the knees, lowering to a 90-degree bend, then returning to a standing position.

Starches - See complex carbohydrates.

Stroke - a sudden loss of brain function caused by blockage or rupture of a blood vessel in the brain.

Success Journal - A book that contains goals, progress updates and orderly workout details to help encourage an individual to continue in his/her workout regimen.

Tendon - A band of tough tissue that connects a muscle to bone.

Teres Major - The muscles found on the upper back, just inside and below the lower deltoids.

Thermic Effect of Food - The amount of energy spent by the metabolic system to digest food and break it down to its nutritional elements.

Time Under Load (TUL) - The amount of time spent performing 1 set of exercise, from the beginning of the first rep to the end of the last.

Training - The process of working the muscles of the body beyond their normal threshold of activity to force growth and adaptation.

Trapezius - The muscles of the upper back, including the inner shoulders and the back of the neck.

Triceps Extension - An exercise in which the palms are face down, clutching a bar and the bar is pushed down from a 90-degree angle in the elbows to a fully extended position and returned to a 90-degree angle. An exercise meant to strengthen the muscles of the triceps.

Triceps - The muscles of the back, upper arms.

TUL - See time under load.

Umbilicus - The naval, located in the center, bottom area of the outer stomach.

Upper Legs Muscle Group - The muscles of the upper legs, including the glutes, hamstrings and quatriceps.

Upper Trapezius - The muscles found on the back of the neck and inner shoulders.

Volume - The amount of work performed during an exercise, including sets, reps, weight and time under load.

Voluntary Action - Conscious muscular movement in which a message is consciously sent through the central nervous system telling a muscle to contract.

Warm-up - Light aerobic exercise at the beginning of a workout to get the blood pumping and prepare the muscles for heavy activity.

Warm-up Sets - Short sets of anaerobic exercise with 50 to 65% of the intended working weight. Warm-up sets are performed to prepare muscles for high intensity weight lifting and to hedge against soreness and injury.

Weight Training - See anaerobic training.

Working Sets - Sets of exercise that are performed until the muscles fail with a full, precalculated amount of weight.

Wrist Extensors - The muscles found on the back of the lower arms that extend the wrist joints.

Wrist Extensors Muscle Group - The muscles found on the back of the lower arms.

Wrist Flexors - The muscles of the inner, forearms that flex the wrist joints.

Wrist Flexors Muscle Group - The muscles found on the front of the lower arms.

APPENDIX B: CALORIC NEED WORKSHEET

CALORIC NEED WORKSHEET

1. CALCULATE YOUR BASAL METABOLIC RATE CALORIC BURN

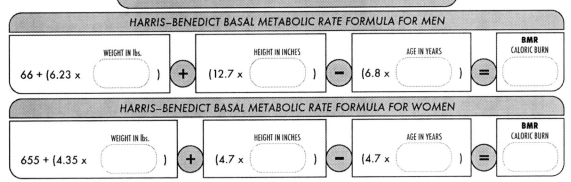

HARRIS–BENEDICT BASAL METABOLIC RATE FORMULA FOR MEN

66 + (6.23 x [WEIGHT IN lbs.]) + (12.7 x [HEIGHT IN INCHES]) − (6.8 x [AGE IN YEARS]) = [BMR CALORIC BURN]

HARRIS–BENEDICT BASAL METABOLIC RATE FORMULA FOR WOMEN

655 + (4.35 x [WEIGHT IN lbs.]) + (4.7 x [HEIGHT IN INCHES]) − (4.7 x [AGE IN YEARS]) = [BMR CALORIC BURN]

2. CALCULATE YOUR ACTIVITY LEVEL CALORIC BURN

ACTIVITY LEVEL	DESCRIPTION	MODIFIER
SEDENTARY	LITTLE TO NO EXERCISE	.2
LIGHTLY ACTIVE	LIGHT EXERCISE SPORTS 1-3 DAYS A WEEK	.375
MODERATELY ACTIVE	MODERATE EXERCISE SPORTS 3-5 DAYS A WEEK	.55
VERY ACTIVE	HARD EXERCISE SPORTS 6-7 DAYS A WEEK	.725
EXTRA ACTIVE	HARD DAILY EXERCISE SPORTS AND A PHYSICAL JOB	.9

[BMR] X [ACTIVITY MODIFIER] = [ACTIVITY CALORIC BURN]

3. CALCULATE YOUR THERMIC EFFECT OF FOOD FOR BMR AND ACTIVITY LEVEL

[BMR CALORIC BURN] + [ACTIVITY CALORIC BURN] X .1 = [THERMIC EFFECT OF FOOD]

4. CALCULATE YOUR TOTAL CALORIC NEED

[BMR CALORIC BURN] + [ACTIVITY CALORIC BURN] + [THERMIC EFFECT OF FOOD CALORIC BURN] = [TOTAL DAILY CALORIC NEED]

APPENDIX C: GOAL WORKSHEET

TOTALhuman
GOALSHEET

NAME _____

DATE _____

Place your current photograph here.

YOUR GOAL #1	PROJECTED ACHIEVEMENT DATE

REASONS FOR SETTING THIS GOAL

_____
_____
_____
_____

YOUR GOAL #2	PROJECTED ACHIEVEMENT DATE

REASONS FOR SETTING THIS GOAL

_____
_____
_____

HOW DO YOU FEEL?

_____
_____
_____
_____
_____
_____
_____
_____
_____
_____
_____
_____

APPENDIX D: PROGRESS MEASUREMENT WORKSHEET

TOTALhuman
PROGRESS MEASUREMENTS

NAME _____

DATE _____

BODY PART	MEASUREMENT
NECK	
SHOULDERS	
CHEST	
LEFT BICEP	
RIGHT BICEP	
LEFT FOREARM	
RIGHT FOREARM	
BELLY	
HIPS	
LEFT THIGH	
RIGHT THIGH	
LEFT CALF	
RIGHT CALF	

SCALE WEIGHT

BODY FAT PERCENTAGE

Place your current photograph here.

SCALE WEIGHT   X   BODY FAT %   =   POUNDS OF BODY FAT

HOW DO YOU FEEL?

Appendix E: Conditioning Worksheet

CONDITIONING WORKSHEET

1. WARM-UP

ACTIVITY	TIME

2. EXERCISES

MUSCLE GROUP	EXERCISE	WEIGHT	REPS	TUL	EVALUATION QUESTIONS
UPPER LEGS	Barbell Squat Cadence (5:2:5) Total Time 12 sec				Are you comfortable with the exercise form? YES ◯ NO ◯ Are you comfortable with the exercise cadence? YES ◯ NO ◯ Are you comfortable performing the exercise? YES ◯ NO ◯ How was the weight? TOO LIGHT ◯ JUST RIGHT ◯ TOO HEAVY ◯ How do you feel after finishing the exercise? NOT FATIGUED ◯ MEDIUM FATIGUE ◯ FATIGUED ◯ HEAVY FATIGUE ◯
UPPER BACK	Barbell Compound Row Cadence (6:2:6) Total Time 14 sec				Are you comfortable with the exercise form? YES ◯ NO ◯ Are you comfortable with the exercise cadence? YES ◯ NO ◯ Are you comfortable performing the exercise? YES ◯ NO ◯ How was the weight? TOO LIGHT ◯ JUST RIGHT ◯ TOO HEAVY ◯ How do you feel after finishing the exercise? NOT FATIGUED ◯ MEDIUM FATIGUE ◯ FATIGUED ◯ HEAVY FATIGUE ◯
LOWER BACK	Barbell Deadlift Cadence (5:2:5) Total Time 12 sec				Are you comfortable with the exercise form? YES ◯ NO ◯ Are you comfortable with the exercise cadence? YES ◯ NO ◯ Are you comfortable performing the exercise? YES ◯ NO ◯ How was the weight? TOO LIGHT ◯ JUST RIGHT ◯ TOO HEAVY ◯ How do you feel after finishing the exercise? NOT FATIGUED ◯ MEDIUM FATIGUE ◯ FATIGUED ◯ HEAVY FATIGUE ◯
CHEST	Barbell Bench Press Cadence (5:2:5) Total Time 12 sec				Are you comfortable with the exercise form? YES ◯ NO ◯ Are you comfortable with the exercise cadence? YES ◯ NO ◯ Are you comfortable performing the exercise? YES ◯ NO ◯ How was the weight? TOO LIGHT ◯ JUST RIGHT ◯ TOO HEAVY ◯ How do you feel after finishing the exercise? NOT FATIGUED ◯ MEDIUM FATIGUE ◯ FATIGUED ◯ HEAVY FATIGUE ◯
SHOULDERS	Barbell Overhead Press Cadence (5:2:5) Total Time 12 sec				Are you comfortable with the exercise form? YES ◯ NO ◯ Are you comfortable with the exercise cadence? YES ◯ NO ◯ Are you comfortable performing the exercise? YES ◯ NO ◯ How was the weight? TOO LIGHT ◯ JUST RIGHT ◯ TOO HEAVY ◯ How do you feel after finishing the exercise? NOT FATIGUED ◯ MEDIUM FATIGUE ◯ FATIGUED ◯ HEAVY FATIGUE ◯
BICEPS	Barbell Preacher Curl Cadence (5:2:5) Total Time 14 sec				Are you comfortable with the exercise form? YES ◯ NO ◯ Are you comfortable with the exercise cadence? YES ◯ NO ◯ Are you comfortable performing the exercise? YES ◯ NO ◯ How was the weight? TOO LIGHT ◯ JUST RIGHT ◯ TOO HEAVY ◯ How do you feel after finishing the exercise? NOT FATIGUED ◯ MEDIUM FATIGUE ◯ FATIGUED ◯ HEAVY FATIGUE ◯

3. COOL-DOWN

ACTIVITY	TIME

4. FLEXIBILITY

MUSCLE GROUP	COMPLETED STRETCH
UPPER LEGS	YES ◯ NO ◯
UPPER BACK	YES ◯ NO ◯
LOWER BACK	YES ◯ NO ◯
CHEST	YES ◯ NO ◯
SHOULDERS	YES ◯ NO ◯
BICEPS	YES ◯ NO ◯

5. EVALUATION

POST-WORKOUT PERSONAL EVALUATION
Are you comfortable with the exercise form? YES ◯ NO ◯
Are you comfortable with the exercise cadence? YES ◯ NO ◯
Are you comfortable performing exercises? YES ◯ NO ◯
How do you feel after the workout? NOT FATIGUED ◯ MEDIUM FATIGUE ◯ FATIGUED ◯ HEAVY FATIGUE ◯

APPENDIX F: FULL BODY WORKOUT SHEET SET

TOTALhuman
FULL-BODY WORKOUT SHEET

NAME _____

DATE _____ WORKOUT # _____

AEROBIC EXERCISE PERFORMED:

TIME:

1. WARM-UP

2. PERFORM EXERCISES

UPPER LEGS

QUADRACEPS

EXERCISE:

CADENCE: WORKING WEIGHT:

	WEIGHT	REPS	TUL	
WARM-UP SET 50%		L R	L R	
WARM-UP SET 65%		L R	L R	LAST WORKOUT / THIS WORKOUT
WORKING SET 100%		L R	L R	
SECOND SET 100%		L R	L R	
THIRD SET 100%		L R	L R	

TAKE A 30 SEC - 2 MIN REST BEFORE PERFORMING THE NEXT EXERCISE

HAMSTRINGS

EXERCISE:

CADENCE: WORKING WEIGHT:

	WEIGHT	REPS	TUL	
WARM-UP SET 50%		L R	L R	
WARM-UP SET 65%		L R	L R	LAST WORKOUT / THIS WORKOUT
WORKING SET 100%		L R	L R	
SECOND SET 100%		L R	L R	
THIRD SET 100%		L R	L R	

TAKE A 30 SEC - 2 MIN REST BEFORE PERFORMING THE NEXT EXERCISE

LOWER LEGS

EXERCISE:

CADENCE: WORKING WEIGHT:

	WEIGHT	REPS	TUL	
WARM-UP SET 50%		L R	L R	
WARM-UP SET 65%		L R	L R	LAST WORKOUT / THIS WORKOUT
WORKING SET 100%		L R	L R	
SECOND SET 100%		L R	L R	
THIRD SET 100%		L R	L R	

TAKE A 30 SEC - 2 MIN REST BEFORE PERFORMING THE NEXT EXERCISE

UPPER BACK

EXERCISE:

CADENCE: WORKING WEIGHT:

	WEIGHT	REPS	TUL	
WARM-UP SET 50%				
WARM-UP SET 65%				LAST WORKOUT / THIS WORKOUT
WORKING SET 100%				
SECOND SET 100%				
THIRD SET 100%				

TAKE A 30 SEC - 2 MIN REST BEFORE PERFORMING THE NEXT EXERCISE

CHEST

EXERCISE:

CADENCE: WORKING WEIGHT:

	WEIGHT	REPS	TUL	
WARM-UP SET 50%				
WARM-UP SET 65%				LAST WORKOUT / THIS WORKOUT
WORKING SET 100%				
SECOND SET 100%				
THIRD SET 100%				

TAKE A 30 SEC - 2 MIN REST BEFORE PERFORMING THE NEXT EXERCISE

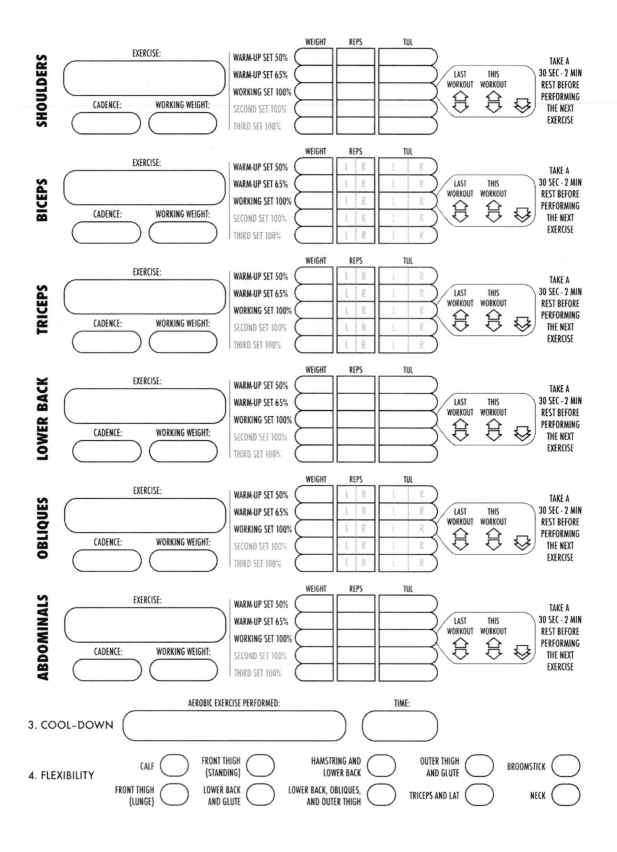

SHOULDERS

EXERCISE:

CADENCE: WORKING WEIGHT:

	WEIGHT	REPS	TUL
WARM-UP SET 50%			
WARM-UP SET 65%			
WORKING SET 100%			
SECOND SET 100%			
THIRD SET 100%			

LAST WORKOUT   THIS WORKOUT

TAKE A 30 SEC - 2 MIN REST BEFORE PERFORMING THE NEXT EXERCISE

BICEPS

EXERCISE:

CADENCE: WORKING WEIGHT:

	WEIGHT		REPS		TUL	
WARM-UP SET 50%			L	R	L	R
WARM-UP SET 65%			L	R	L	R
WORKING SET 100%			L	R	L	R
SECOND SET 100%			L	R	L	R
THIRD SET 100%			L	R	L	R

LAST WORKOUT   THIS WORKOUT

TAKE A 30 SEC - 2 MIN REST BEFORE PERFORMING THE NEXT EXERCISE

TRICEPS

EXERCISE:

CADENCE: WORKING WEIGHT:

	WEIGHT		REPS		TUL	
WARM-UP SET 50%			L	R	L	R
WARM-UP SET 65%			L	R	L	R
WORKING SET 100%			L	R	L	R
SECOND SET 100%			L	R	L	R
THIRD SET 100%			L	R	L	R

LAST WORKOUT   THIS WORKOUT

TAKE A 30 SEC - 2 MIN REST BEFORE PERFORMING THE NEXT EXERCISE

LOWER BACK

EXERCISE:

CADENCE: WORKING WEIGHT:

	WEIGHT	REPS	TUL
WARM-UP SET 50%			
WARM-UP SET 65%			
WORKING SET 100%			
SECOND SET 100%			
THIRD SET 100%			

LAST WORKOUT   THIS WORKOUT

TAKE A 30 SEC - 2 MIN REST BEFORE PERFORMING THE NEXT EXERCISE

OBLIQUES

EXERCISE:

CADENCE: WORKING WEIGHT:

	WEIGHT		REPS		TUL	
WARM-UP SET 50%			L	R	L	R
WARM-UP SET 65%			L	R	L	R
WORKING SET 100%			L	R	L	R
SECOND SET 100%			L	R	L	R
THIRD SET 100%			L	R	L	R

LAST WORKOUT   THIS WORKOUT

TAKE A 30 SEC - 2 MIN REST BEFORE PERFORMING THE NEXT EXERCISE

ABDOMINALS

EXERCISE:

CADENCE: WORKING WEIGHT:

	WEIGHT	REPS	TUL
WARM-UP SET 50%			
WARM-UP SET 65%			
WORKING SET 100%			
SECOND SET 100%			
THIRD SET 100%			

LAST WORKOUT   THIS WORKOUT

TAKE A 30 SEC - 2 MIN REST BEFORE PERFORMING THE NEXT EXERCISE

3. COOL-DOWN

AEROBIC EXERCISE PERFORMED: TIME:

4. FLEXIBILITY

CALF

FRONT THIGH (STANDING)

HAMSTRING AND LOWER BACK

OUTER THIGH AND GLUTE

BROOMSTICK

FRONT THIGH (LUNGE)

LOWER BACK AND GLUTE

LOWER BACK, OBLIQUES, AND OUTER THIGH

TRICEPS AND LAT

NECK

APPENDIX G: 2-DAY BREAKOUT WORKOUT SHEET SET

2 DAY BREAKOUT SHEET - A

NAME _____

DATE _____ WORKOUT # _____

1. WARM-UP

AEROBIC EXERCISE PERFORMED:

TIME:

2. PERFORM EXERCISES

UPPER LEGS

QUADRACEPS

EXERCISE:

CADENCE: | WORKING WEIGHT:

	WEIGHT	REPS	TUL
WARM-UP SET 50%		L R	L R
WARM-UP SET 65%		L R	L R
WORKING SET 100%		L R	L R
SECOND SET 100%		L R	L R
THIRD SET 100%		L R	L R

LAST WORKOUT | THIS WORKOUT

TAKE A 30 SEC - 2 MIN REST BEFORE PERFORMING THE NEXT EXERCISE

HAMSTRINGS

EXERCISE:

CADENCE: | WORKING WEIGHT:

	WEIGHT	REPS	TUL
WARM-UP SET 50%		L R	L R
WARM-UP SET 65%		L R	L R
WORKING SET 100%		L R	L R
SECOND SET 100%		L R	L R
THIRD SET 100%		L R	L R

LAST WORKOUT | THIS WORKOUT

TAKE A 30 SEC - 2 MIN REST BEFORE PERFORMING THE NEXT EXERCISE

LOWER LEGS

EXERCISE:

CADENCE: | WORKING WEIGHT:

	WEIGHT	REPS	TUL
WARM-UP SET 50%		L R	L R
WARM-UP SET 65%		L R	L R
WORKING SET 100%		L R	L R
SECOND SET 100%		L R	L R
THIRD SET 100%		L R	L R

LAST WORKOUT | THIS WORKOUT

TAKE A 30 SEC - 2 MIN REST BEFORE PERFORMING THE NEXT EXERCISE

UPPER BACK

EXERCISE:

CADENCE: | WORKING WEIGHT:

	WEIGHT	REPS	TUL
WARM-UP SET 50%			
WARM-UP SET 65%			
WORKING SET 100%			
SECOND SET 100%			
THIRD SET 100%			

LAST WORKOUT | THIS WORKOUT

TAKE A 30 SEC - 2 MIN REST BEFORE PERFORMING THE NEXT EXERCISE

2 DAY BREAKOUT SHEET - A (continued)

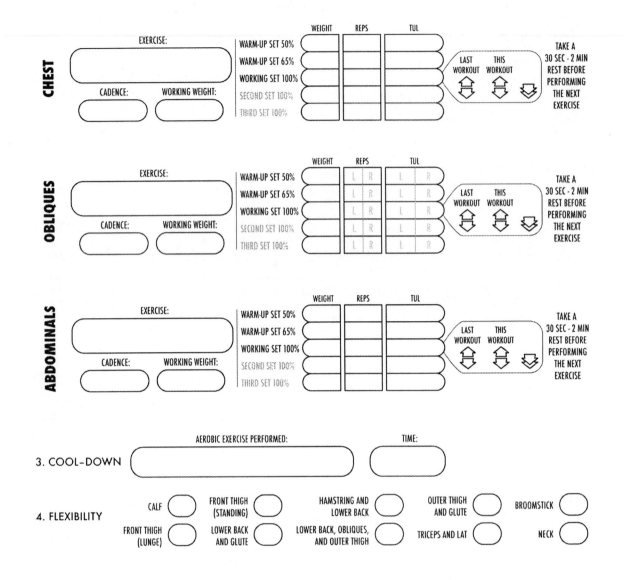

CHEST

EXERCISE:

CADENCE: WORKING WEIGHT:

	WEIGHT	REPS	TUL
WARM-UP SET 50%			
WARM-UP SET 65%			
WORKING SET 100%			
SECOND SET 100%			
THIRD SET 100%			

LAST WORKOUT   THIS WORKOUT

TAKE A 30 SEC - 2 MIN REST BEFORE PERFORMING THE NEXT EXERCISE

OBLIQUES

EXERCISE:

CADENCE: WORKING WEIGHT:

	WEIGHT	REPS		TUL	
		L	R	L	R
WARM-UP SET 50%		L	R	L	R
WARM-UP SET 65%		L	R	L	R
WORKING SET 100%		L	R	L	R
SECOND SET 100%		L	R	L	R
THIRD SET 100%		L	R	L	R

LAST WORKOUT   THIS WORKOUT

TAKE A 30 SEC - 2 MIN REST BEFORE PERFORMING THE NEXT EXERCISE

ABDOMINALS

EXERCISE:

CADENCE: WORKING WEIGHT:

	WEIGHT	REPS	TUL
WARM-UP SET 50%			
WARM-UP SET 65%			
WORKING SET 100%			
SECOND SET 100%			
THIRD SET 100%			

LAST WORKOUT   THIS WORKOUT

TAKE A 30 SEC - 2 MIN REST BEFORE PERFORMING THE NEXT EXERCISE

3. COOL-DOWN

AEROBIC EXERCISE PERFORMED: TIME:

4. FLEXIBILITY

CALF ◯   FRONT THIGH (STANDING) ◯   HAMSTRING AND LOWER BACK ◯   OUTER THIGH AND GLUTE ◯   BROOMSTICK ◯

FRONT THIGH (LUNGE) ◯   LOWER BACK AND GLUTE ◯   LOWER BACK, OBLIQUES, AND OUTER THIGH ◯   TRICEPS AND LAT ◯   NECK ◯

172

2 DAY BREAKOUT SHEET - B

NAME _____

DATE _____ WORKOUT # _____

AEROBIC EXERCISE PERFORMED: TIME:

1. WARM–UP

2. PERFORM EXERCISES

TRICEPS

EXERCISE:

CADENCE: WORKING WEIGHT:

	WEIGHT	REPS	TUL
WARM-UP SET 50%		L R	L R
WARM-UP SET 65%		L R	L R
WORKING SET 100%		L R	L R
SECOND SET 100%		L R	L R
THIRD SET 100%		L R	L R

LAST WORKOUT   THIS WORKOUT

TAKE A 30 SEC - 2 MIN REST BEFORE PERFORMING THE NEXT EXERCISE

SHOULDERS

EXERCISE:

CADENCE: WORKING WEIGHT:

	WEIGHT	REPS	TUL
WARM-UP SET 50%			
WARM-UP SET 65%			
WORKING SET 100%			
SECOND SET 100%			
THIRD SET 100%			

LAST WORKOUT   THIS WORKOUT

TAKE A 30 SEC - 2 MIN REST BEFORE PERFORMING THE NEXT EXERCISE

TRAPEZIUS

EXERCISE:

CADENCE: WORKING WEIGHT:

	WEIGHT	REPS	TUL
WARM-UP SET 50%			
WARM-UP SET 65%			
WORKING SET 100%			
SECOND SET 100%			
THIRD SET 100%			

LAST WORKOUT   THIS WORKOUT

TAKE A 30 SEC - 2 MIN REST BEFORE PERFORMING THE NEXT EXERCISE

2 DAY BREAKOUT SHEET - B (continued)

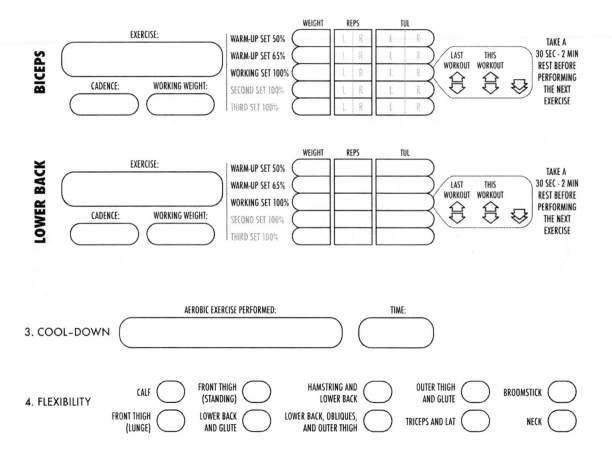

BICEPS

EXERCISE:

CADENCE: WORKING WEIGHT:

	WEIGHT	REPS		TUL	
		L	R	L	R
WARM-UP SET 50%					
WARM-UP SET 65%					
WORKING SET 100%					
SECOND SET 100%					
THIRD SET 100%					

LAST WORKOUT   THIS WORKOUT

TAKE A 30 SEC - 2 MIN REST BEFORE PERFORMING THE NEXT EXERCISE

LOWER BACK

EXERCISE:

CADENCE: WORKING WEIGHT:

	WEIGHT	REPS	TUL
WARM-UP SET 50%			
WARM-UP SET 65%			
WORKING SET 100%			
SECOND SET 100%			
THIRD SET 100%			

LAST WORKOUT   THIS WORKOUT

TAKE A 30 SEC - 2 MIN REST BEFORE PERFORMING THE NEXT EXERCISE

3. COOL-DOWN

AEROBIC EXERCISE PERFORMED:

TIME:

4. FLEXIBILITY

CALF ◯

FRONT THIGH (STANDING) ◯

HAMSTRING AND LOWER BACK ◯

OUTER THIGH AND GLUTE ◯

BROOMSTICK ◯

FRONT THIGH (LUNGE) ◯

LOWER BACK AND GLUTE ◯

LOWER BACK, OBLIQUES, AND OUTER THIGH ◯

TRICEPS AND LAT ◯

NECK ◯

APPENDIX H: 3-DAY BREAKOUT WORKOUT SHEET SET

3 DAY BREAKOUT SHEET - A

NAME _____

DATE _____ WORKOUT # _____

1. WARM-UP

AEROBIC EXERCISE PERFORMED:

TIME:

2. PERFORM EXERCISES

UPPER LEGS

QUADRACEPS

EXERCISE:

CADENCE: WORKING WEIGHT:

	WEIGHT	REPS	TUL
WARM-UP SET 50%		L R	L R
WARM-UP SET 65%		L R	L R
WORKING SET 100%		L R	L R
SECOND SET 100%		L R	L R
THIRD SET 100%		L R	L R

LAST WORKOUT   THIS WORKOUT

TAKE A 30 SEC - 2 MIN REST BEFORE PERFORMING THE NEXT EXERCISE

HAMSTRINGS

EXERCISE:

CADENCE: WORKING WEIGHT:

	WEIGHT	REPS	TUL
WARM-UP SET 50%		L R	L R
WARM-UP SET 65%		L R	L R
WORKING SET 100%		L R	L R
SECOND SET 100%		L R	L R
THIRD SET 100%		L R	L R

LAST WORKOUT   THIS WORKOUT

TAKE A 30 SEC - 2 MIN REST BEFORE PERFORMING THE NEXT EXERCISE

LOWER LEGS

EXERCISE:

CADENCE: WORKING WEIGHT:

	WEIGHT	REPS	TUL
WARM-UP SET 50%		L R	L R
WARM-UP SET 65%		L R	L R
WORKING SET 100%		L R	L R
SECOND SET 100%		L R	L R
THIRD SET 100%		L R	L R

LAST WORKOUT   THIS WORKOUT

TAKE A 30 SEC - 2 MIN REST BEFORE PERFORMING THE NEXT EXERCISE

OBLIQUES

EXERCISE:

CADENCE: WORKING WEIGHT:

	WEIGHT	REPS	TUL
WARM-UP SET 50%			
WARM-UP SET 65%			
WORKING SET 100%			
SECOND SET 100%			
THIRD SET 100%			

LAST WORKOUT   THIS WORKOUT

TAKE A 30 SEC - 2 MIN REST BEFORE PERFORMING THE NEXT EXERCISE

ABDOMINALS

EXERCISE:

CADENCE: WORKING WEIGHT:

	WEIGHT	REPS	TUL
WARM-UP SET 50%			
WARM-UP SET 65%			
WORKING SET 100%			
SECOND SET 100%			
THIRD SET 100%			

LAST WORKOUT   THIS WORKOUT

TAKE A 30 SEC - 2 MIN REST BEFORE PERFORMING THE NEXT EXERCISE

3. COOL-DOWN

AEROBIC EXERCISE PERFORMED:

TIME:

4. FLEXIBILITY

CALF

FRONT THIGH (STANDING)

HAMSTRING AND LOWER BACK

OUTER THIGH AND GLUTE

BROOMSTICK

FRONT THIGH (LUNGE)

LOWER BACK AND GLUTE

LOWER BACK, OBLIQUES, AND OUTER THIGH

TRICEPS AND LAT

NECK

3 DAY BREAKOUT SHEET - B

NAME _____

DATE _____ WORKOUT # _____

AEROBIC EXERCISE PERFORMED: TIME:

1. WARM-UP

2. PERFORM EXERCISES

UPPER BACK

EXERCISE:

CADENCE: WORKING WEIGHT:

	WEIGHT	REPS	TUL
WARM-UP SET 50%			
WARM-UP SET 65%			
WORKING SET 100%			
SECOND SET 100%			
THIRD SET 100%			

LAST WORKOUT   THIS WORKOUT

TAKE A 30 SEC - 2 MIN REST BEFORE PERFORMING THE NEXT EXERCISE

LOWER BACK

EXERCISE:

CADENCE: WORKING WEIGHT:

	WEIGHT	REPS	TUL
WARM-UP SET 50%			
WARM-UP SET 65%			
WORKING SET 100%			
SECOND SET 100%			
THIRD SET 100%			

LAST WORKOUT   THIS WORKOUT

TAKE A 30 SEC - 2 MIN REST BEFORE PERFORMING THE NEXT EXERCISE

BICEPS

EXERCISE:

CADENCE: WORKING WEIGHT:

	WEIGHT	REPS		TUL	
		L	R	L	R
WARM-UP SET 50%		L	R	L	R
WARM-UP SET 65%		L	R	L	R
WORKING SET 100%		L	R	L	R
SECOND SET 100%		L	R	L	R
THIRD SET 100%		L	R	L	R

LAST WORKOUT   THIS WORKOUT

TAKE A 30 SEC - 2 MIN REST BEFORE PERFORMING THE NEXT EXERCISE

WRIST FLEXORS

EXERCISE:

CADENCE: WORKING WEIGHT:

	WEIGHT	REPS		TUL	
		L	R	L	R
WARM-UP SET 50%					
WARM-UP SET 65%					
WORKING SET 100%					
SECOND SET 100%					
THIRD SET 100%					

LAST WORKOUT   THIS WORKOUT

TAKE A 30 SEC - 2 MIN REST BEFORE PERFORMING THE NEXT EXERCISE

WRIST EXTENSORS

EXERCISE:

CADENCE: WORKING WEIGHT:

	WEIGHT	REPS		TUL	
		L	R	L	R
WARM-UP SET 50%					
WARM-UP SET 65%					
WORKING SET 100%					
SECOND SET 100%					
THIRD SET 100%					

LAST WORKOUT   THIS WORKOUT

TAKE A 30 SEC - 2 MIN REST BEFORE PERFORMING THE NEXT EXERCISE

3. COOL-DOWN

AEROBIC EXERCISE PERFORMED: TIME:

4. FLEXIBILITY

CALF ◯   FRONT THIGH (STANDING) ◯   HAMSTRING AND LOWER BACK ◯   OUTER THIGH AND GLUTE ◯   BROOMSTICK ◯

FRONT THIGH (LUNGE) ◯   LOWER BACK AND GLUTE ◯   LOWER BACK, OBLIQUES, AND OUTER THIGH ◯   TRICEPS AND LAT ◯   NECK ◯

3 DAY BREAKOUT SHEET - C

NAME _____

DATE _____ WORKOUT # _____

1. WARM-UP

AEROBIC EXERCISE PERFORMED:

TIME:

2. PERFORM EXERCISES

CHEST

EXERCISE:

CADENCE: WORKING WEIGHT:

	WEIGHT	REPS	TUL
WARM-UP SET 50%			
WARM-UP SET 65%			
WORKING SET 100%			
SECOND SET 100%			
THIRD SET 100%			

LAST WORKOUT   THIS WORKOUT

TAKE A 30 SEC - 2 MIN REST BEFORE PERFORMING THE NEXT EXERCISE

SHOULDERS

EXERCISE:

CADENCE: WORKING WEIGHT:

	WEIGHT	REPS	TUL
WARM-UP SET 50%			
WARM-UP SET 65%			
WORKING SET 100%			
SECOND SET 100%			
THIRD SET 100%			

LAST WORKOUT   THIS WORKOUT

TAKE A 30 SEC - 2 MIN REST BEFORE PERFORMING THE NEXT EXERCISE

TRAPEZIUS

EXERCISE:

CADENCE: WORKING WEIGHT:

	WEIGHT	REPS	TUL
WARM-UP SET 50%			
WARM-UP SET 65%			
WORKING SET 100%			
SECOND SET 100%			
THIRD SET 100%			

LAST WORKOUT   THIS WORKOUT

TAKE A 30 SEC - 2 MIN REST BEFORE PERFORMING THE NEXT EXERCISE

TRICEPS

EXERCISE:

CADENCE: WORKING WEIGHT:

	WEIGHT	REPS		TUL	
		L	R	L	R
WARM-UP SET 50%					
WARM-UP SET 65%					
WORKING SET 100%					
SECOND SET 100%					
THIRD SET 100%					

LAST WORKOUT   THIS WORKOUT

TAKE A 30 SEC - 2 MIN REST BEFORE PERFORMING THE NEXT EXERCISE

3. COOL-DOWN

AEROBIC EXERCISE PERFORMED:

TIME:

4. FLEXIBILITY

CALF ◯

FRONT THIGH (STANDING) ◯

HAMSTRING AND LOWER BACK ◯

OUTER THIGH AND GLUTE ◯

BROOMSTICK ◯

FRONT THIGH (LUNGE) ◯

LOWER BACK AND GLUTE ◯

LOWER BACK, OBLIQUES, AND OUTER THIGH ◯

TRICEPS AND LAT ◯

NECK ◯

APPENDIX I: EXERCISES

MUSCLE GROUP - UPPER BACK	**CADENCE - 6:2:6**
EXERCISE - BARBELL COMPOUND ROW	**REQUIRED EQUIPMENT -** BARBELL

Begin this exercise with a loaded barbell in deadlift position with a high chest and tight back. Concentrating on the upper back muscles, lift the barbell over a 6-second count to a contracted position.

Hold in a fully contracted position with the elbows bent to 90-degree angles for a full 2-second count.

Concentrating on the muscles in the upper back, lower the barbell back to starting position over a full 6-second count.

MUSCLE GROUP - UPPER BACK	**CADENCE - 6:2:6**
EXERCISE - DUMBBELL ONE-ARM ROW	**REQUIRED EQUIPMENT -** DUMBBELLS, BENCH

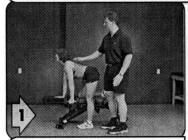  

Begin this exercise with one dumbbell and the opposing knee on a bench. Over a full 6-second count, concentrating on the upper back muscles, lift the dumbbell till your elbow is at a 90-degree angle.

Hold in a fully contracted position for a 2-second count.

Concentrating on the muscles of the upper back, lower the dumbbell over a 6-second count to the starting position.

MUSCLE GROUP - LOWER BACK	**CADENCE - 5:2:5**
EXERCISE - BARBELL DEADLIFT	**REQUIRED EQUIPMENT -** BARBELL

Concentrating on the muscles in the lower back, descend to the bottom position in a full 5-second count. Make sure to keep the chest high and the back straight.

Remain in the bottom position for a 2-second count.

Concentrating on the muscles in your lower back, move to the starting position over a 5-second count.

MUSCLE GROUP - LOWER BACK	CADENCE - 10:2:5
EXERCISE - LOWER BACK EXTENSIONS	REQUIRED EQUIPMENT - PLATE, BACK EXTENSION BENCH

Taking a weight-plate and clutching it to your chest, begin this exercise by concentrating the muscles of the lower back and extending to a fully contracted position over a full 10-second count.

Remain at a fully contracted position for a full 2-second count.

Concentrating on the muscles in the lower back, move back to the beginning position over a full 5-second count.

MUSCLE GROUP - UPPER LEGS	CADENCE - 5:2:5
EXERCISE - BARBELL SQUAT	REQUIRED EQUIPMENT - BARBELL

Begin this exercise with a loaded barbell held over the shoulders in a standing position. Concentrating on the upper leg muscles, squat with a high chest and tight back muscles over a full 5-second count to the bottom position.

Hold in the bottom position for a full 2-second count.

Concentrating on the muscles of the upper legs, move back to the starting position over a full 5-second count.

MUSCLE GROUP - UPPER LEGS	CADENCE - 5:2:5
EXERCISE - LYING MACHINE PRESS	REQUIRED EQUIPMENT - LEG MACHINE PRESS

Begin this exercise with legs fully extended, supporting the weight. Concentrating on the upper leg muscles, lower the weight over a full 5-second count to the bottom position.

Hold in the bottom position with the knees bent to about 90 degree angles for a full 2-second count.

Concentrating on the muscles of the upper legs, push the weight back to the starting position over a full 5-second count.

MUSCLE GROUP - LOWER LEGS	CADENCE - 5:2:5
EXERCISE - DUMBBELL STANDING CALF RAISE	REQUIRED EQUIPMENT - DUMBBELLS

Begin this exercise with a dumbbell in one hand. Cross one ankle over the other. Concentrating on the muscles of the calf, roll up onto the toes into a fully extended position over a full 5-second count.	Remain in an extended position for a full 2-second count	Concentrating on the muscles of the calf, descend back to the opening position over a full 5-second count. Perform this exercise one leg at a time. This exercise may be performed on stairs in your home.

MUSCLE GROUP - LOWER LEGS	CADENCE - 5:2:5
EXERCISE - MACHINE SITTING CALF RAISE	REQUIRED EQUIPMENT - SITTING CALF RAISE MACHINE

Begin this exercise with the heels down, the weight resting on the knees. Concentrating on the muscles of the calves, roll up onto the toes into a fully extended position over a full 5-second count.	Remain in a fully extended position for a full 2-second count.	Concentrating on the muscles of the calves, roll back to the beginning position over a full 5-second count.

MUSCLE GROUP - BICEPS	CADENCE - 6:2:6
EXERCISE - BARBELL PREACHER CURL	REQUIRED EQUIPMENT - BARBELL, PREACHER CURL BENCH

Taking a loaded barbell, begin this exercise at the top position of the movement. Concentrating on the muscles in the biceps, over a full 6-second count lower the barbell to the bottom position.	Remain in the bottom position for a full 2-second count.	Concentrating on the muscles in the biceps, return to the starting position over a full 6-second count.

MUSCLE GROUP - BICEPS	CADENCE - 6:2:6
EXERCISE - DUMBBELL CURL	REQUIRED EQUIPMENT - DUMBBELLS

1	2	3
Taking two dumbbells, one in each hand, begin this exercise at the top position just short of elbow lock out. Concentrating on the bicep muscles, lower the dumbbells to a 90-degree angle over a full 6-second count.	Hold in the bottom position with both elbows at 90-degree angles for a full 2-second count.	Concentrating on the muscles of the biceps, return to the starting position over a full 6-second count.

MUSCLE GROUP - TRICEPS	CADENCE - 5:2:5
EXERCISE - CABLE TRICEP EXTENSION	REQUIRED EQUIPMENT - CABLE TRICEP EXTENSION MACHINE

1	2	3
Begin this exercise in a fully extended position. Concentrating on the muscles of the triceps, over a full 5-second count, raise the bar until both elbows are at 90-degree angles.	Remain at a 90-degree angle for a full 2-second count.	Concentrating on the muscles of the triceps, push the bar back down to the starting position over a full 5-second count.

MUSCLE GROUP - TRICEPS	CADENCE - 5:2:5
EXERCISE - DUMBBELL OVERHEAD EXTENSIONS	REQUIRED EQUIPMENT - DUMBBELLS, BENCH

  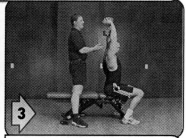

1	2	3
Begin this exercise with a single dumbbell held flat-palmed, extended above your head. Concentrating on the muscles of the triceps, lower the dumbbell to the bottom position over a full 5-second count.	Hold at the bottom position with the elbows bent to 90-degree angles for a full 2-second count.	Concentrating on the muscles of the triceps, extend the dumbbell back to the starting position over a full 5-second count.

MUSCLE GROUP - ABDOMINALS	CADENCE - 5:2:5
EXERCISE - MACHINE ABDOMINAL CRUNCH	REQUIRED EQUIPMENT - AB CRUNCH MACHINE

Begin this exercise by sitting in an abdominal crunch machine and clipping on the seat belt. Driving with the elbows, contract the abdominal muscles to pull the handles of the machine forward over a full 5-second count.	Hold in a fully contracted position for a full 2-second count.	Concentrating on the abdominal muscles, move back to the starting position over a full 5-second count.

MUSCLE GROUP - ABDOMINALS	CADENCE - 5:2:5
EXERCISE - INCLINE BENCH AB CRUNCH	REQUIRED EQUIPMENT - INCLINE BENCH, WEIGHT PLATE

Start this exercise in the top position of the crunch and clutching a weight plate against the chest. Concentrating on the abdominal muscles, descend to the bottom position over a full 5-second count.	Hold in the bottom position for a full 2-second count.	Concentrating on the abdominal muscles, move back to the starting position over a full 5-second count.

MUSCLE GROUP - OBLIQUES	CADENCE - 5:2:5
EXERCISE - TORSO ROTATION	REQUIRED EQUIPMENT - TORSO ROTATION MACHINE

Begin this exercise by sitting in a torso rotation machine. Concentrating on the oblique muscles, rotate the upper body to a fully contracted position over a full 5-second count.	Hold in a fully contracted position for a full 2-seconds.	Move back to the beginning position over a full 5-second count, concentrating on the oblique muscles.

MUSCLE GROUP - OBLIQUES	CADENCE - 5:2:5
EXERCISE - DUMBBELL SIDE BENDS	REQUIRED EQUIPMENT - DUMBBELLS

Begin this exercise by taking a dumbbell in one hand and standing straight. Concentrating on the oblique muscles, move to the bottom position over a full 5-second count by bending the waist towards the weight.	Hold in the bottom position for a full 2-second count.	Concentrating on the oblique muscles, move back to the beginning position of the exercise over a full 5-second count.

MUSCLE GROUP - SHOULDERS	CADENCE - 5:2:5
EXERCISE - BARBELL OVERHEAD PRESS	REQUIRED EQUIPMENT - BARBELL

Begin this exercise in a sitting position with a loaded barbell held over the head. Concentrating on the shoulder muscles, move the barbell down to the bottom position of the exercise over a full 5-second count.	Hold in the bottom position with the elbows at 90-degree angles for a full 2-second count.	Concentrating on the shoulder muscles, move to the starting position over a full 5-second count.

MUSCLE GROUP - SHOULDERS	CADENCE - 5:2:5
EXERCISE - DUMBBELL LATERAL RAISE	REQUIRED EQUIPMENT - DUMBBELLS

Begin this exercise holding two dumbbells. Concentrating on the muscles of the shoulders, raise the dumbbells to the top position over a full 5-second count.	Hold in the top position for a full 2-second count.	Concentrating on the muscles of the shoulders, lower the dumbbells back to the starting position over a full 5-second count.

MUSCLE GROUP - CHEST

EXERCISE - BARBELL BENCH PRESS

CADENCE - 5:2:5

REQUIRED EQUIPMENT - BARBELL, BENCH PRESS

Using a loaded barbell, begin this exercise at the top of the movement with the arms just short of lock-out. Concentrating on the muscles of the chest, lower the barbell over a full 5-second count until your elbows are at 90-degree angles.

Hold in the bottom position with the elbows at 90-degree angles for a full 2-second count.

Concentrating on the muscles of the chest, move to the starting position of the exercise over a full 5-second count.

MUSCLE GROUP - CHEST

EXERCISE - DUMBBELL FLIES

CADENCE - 5:2:5

REQUIRED EQUIPMENT - DUMBBELLS, BENCH

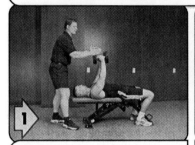  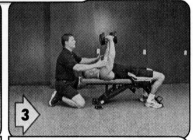

Using 2 dumbbells, begin this exercise at the top of the movement. Concentrating on the muscles of the chest and with slightly bent elbows, lower the arms to the sides over a full 5-second count.

Hold at the bottom position with the arms extended out to the sides for a full 2-second count.

Concentrating on the muscles of the chest, return to the starting position of the exercise over a full 5-second count.

MUSCLE GROUP - TRAPEZIUS

EXERCISE - DUMBBELL SHOULDER SHRUGS

CADENCE - 3:2:3

REQUIRED EQUIPMENT - DUMBBELLS

Begin this exercise with 2 dumbbells held to the sides. Concentrating on the muscles of the trapezius, shrug the shoulders up to a fully contracted position over a full 3-second count.

Hold in a fully contracted position for a full 2-second count.

Concentrating on the muscles of the trapezius, lower the dumbbells back to the starting position of the exercise over a full 3-second count.

MUSCLE GROUP - TRAPEZIUS	CADENCE - 3:2:3
EXERCISE - BARBELL SHOULDER SHRUGS	REQUIRED EQUIPMENT - BARBELL

Begin this exercise with a loaded barbell and in a standing position. Concentrating on the muscles of the trapezius, shrug the shoulders to raise the weight to a fully contracted position over a full 3-second count.

Hold in a fully contracted position for a full 2-second count.

Concentrating on the muscles of the trapezius, move the barbell back to the starting position of the exercise over a full 3-second count.

MUSCLE GROUP - REAR DELTOIDS	CADENCE - 5:2:5
EXERCISE - DUMBBELL BENT RAISES	REQUIRED EQUIPMENT - DUMBBELLS, BENCH

Begin this exercise by sitting, bent over, with 2 dumbbells. Concentrating on the muscles on the backs of the shoulders, raise the dumbbells to the top position over a full 5-second count.

Hold in the top position for a full 2-second count.

Concentrating on the muscles on the backs of the shoulders, lower the dumbbells to a 45 degree angle over a full 5-second count.

MUSCLE GROUP - REAR DELTOIDS	CADENCE - 5:2:5
EXERCISE - CABLE BENT LATERALS	REQUIRED EQUIPMENT - CABLE MACHINE

Begin this exercise bent over with two cables pulling from opposing directions. Concentrating on the muscles on the back of the shoulders, raise to the top position over a full 5-second count.

Hold in the top position for a full 2-second count.

Concentrating on the muscles on the back of the shoulders, move to the starting position of the exercise over a full 5-second count.

MUSCLE GROUP - WRIST EXTENSORS

CADENCE - 3:2:3

EXERCISE - BARBELL REVERSE WRIST CURLS

REQUIRED EQUIPMENT - BARBELL

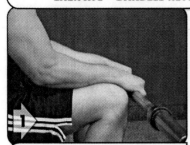  

Begin this exercise with a barbell, relaxed on the knees. Concentrating on the wrist extensor muscles, bring the barbell up to the top position over a full 3-second count.

Hold in the top position for a full 2-second count.

Concentrating on the wrist extensors and over a full 3-second count, move the weight back to the starting position.

MUSCLE GROUP - WRIST FLEXORS

CADENCE - 3:2:3

EXERCISE - DUMBBELL WRIST CURLS

REQUIRED EQUIPMENT - DUMBBELLS

Begin this exercise holding 2 dumbbells on the knees. Concentrating on the wrist flexors, curl the weight to the top position over a full 3-second count.

Hold in the top position for a full 2-second count.

Concentrating on the wrist flexors and over a full 3-second count, move the weight back to the beginning position.

APPENDIX J: STRETCHING EXERCISES

Calf Stretch
Muscles stretched: Calves

Use a wall to stabilize yourself. Standing in a split legged position with your left foot back and your right foot forward, apply pressure to your left foot until you feel the muscles of your left calf stretch. Hold this position for 3 sets of 10 seconds each. Repeat this stretch for the right leg.

Front Thigh Stretch
Muscles stretched: Quadriceps

From a standing position, lift your right foot behind you. Use your right hand to pull your right heel towards your buttocks until you feel the muscles of your right front thigh stretch. If needed, use a wall or rail to stabilize yourself. Hold this position for 3 sets of 10 seconds each. Repeat this stretch for the left leg.

Hamstring and Lower Back Stretch
Muscles stretched: Hamstrings and
Erector Spinae

Place your right heel on a stable platform like a rail or table. Lock the knee and lean forward, bending your lower back until you feel the muscles of your right hamstring and lower back stretch. Hold this position for 3 sets of 10 seconds each. Repeat this stretch for the left leg.

Outer Thigh and Glute Stretch
Muscles stretched: Outer Thigh and Glutes

From a sitting position, bend the right knee and place your right foot on the outside of your left knee in a cross-legged position. Using your right hand, push your right knee across your body until you feel the muscles of your right glute and thigh stretch. Hold this position for 3 sets of 10 seconds each. Repeat this stretch for the left leg.

Front Thigh Stretch
Muscles Stretched: Quadriceps

Step forward with your left foot into a lunge position. Lower your body until you are over your bent left knee and your palms are against the floor. Rock your left foot back on the toe until you feel the muscles of your right hip and thigh stretch. Hold this position for 3 sets of 10 seconds each. Repeat this stretch for the left leg.

Lower Back and Glute Stretch
Muscles stretched: Gluteus, Erector Spinea, and Hip Muscles

While lying on your back. Use your hands to draw your right knee to your chest until you feel the muscles of your lower back and glute stretch. Hold this position for 3 sets of 10 seconds each. Repeat this stretch for the other leg.

Lower Back, Obliques, and Outer Thigh Stretch
Erector Spinae, Obliques and Outer Thigh

While lying on your back, bend your right knee and place your right foot on the outside of your left knee in a cross-legged position. Using your left hand, pull the right knee across your body until you feel the muscles of your right oblique and outer thigh stretch. Hold this position for 3 sets of 10 seconds each.

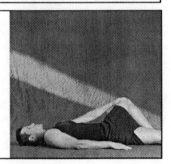

Triceps and Lat Stretch
Muscles stretched: Triceps, Latissimus Dorsi and Obliques

While standing, bend your right elbow and hold it with your left hand. Use your left hand to draw your right elbow inward, behind your head until you feel the muscles of your triceps and lats stretch. Hold this position for 3 sets of 10 seconds each. Repeat this stretch with the left arm.

Broomstick Stretch
Muscles stretched: Anterior Deltoids, Biceps and Pectoral

From a standing position, hold a broomstick with an underhanded grip behind your back. Raise the broomstick behind your back until you feel the muscles of your pecs, anterior deltoids and biceps stretch. Hold this position for 3 sets of 10 seconds each.

Neck Stretch
Muscles stretched: Trapezius

While standing, tilt your head to the left, looking straight forward, until you feel the muscles of your right trapezius stretch. Hold this position for 3 sets of 10 seconds each. Repeat this exercise for the left trapezius.

APPENDIX K: BODY MEASUREMENTS

BODY MEASUREMENTS

NECK

Wrap a measuring tape just below the Adams apple for men or midway between the chin and the shoulders for women.

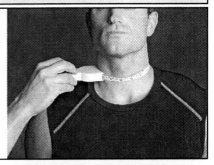

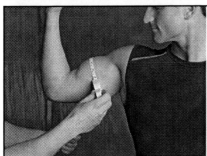

UPPER ARM

Wrap a measuring tape in a straight line around the largest area of the upper arm. Hold the arm parallel to the floor and flex while taking the measurement.

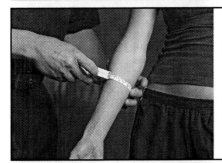

FOREARM

Extend the elbow completely. Make a fist to flex the forearm. Wrap a measuring tape in a straight line around the largest part of the forearm.

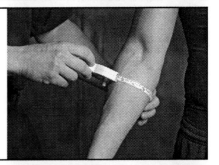

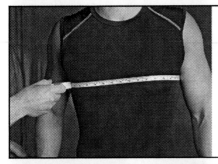

CHEST

With the shoulders squared, stand upright and measure around the torso with the tape running in a horizontal line over the nipples.

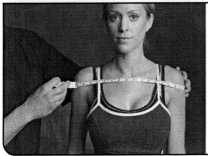

SHOULDERS

With the shoulders squared, stand upright and measure around the shoulders with the tape running in a horizontal line around the largest part of the shoulder area.

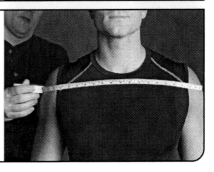

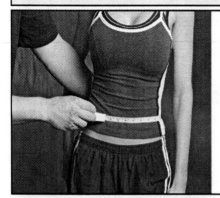

WAIST

Wrap a measuring tape in a horizontal line around the waist at the level of the navel.

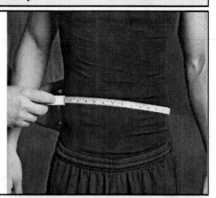

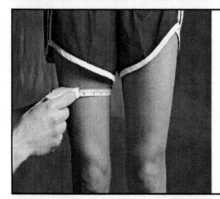

HIPS

Stand straight up with the heels together and with your weight evenly distributed on both feet. Wrap a measuring tape in a horizontal line around the hips at the largest point of the glutes.

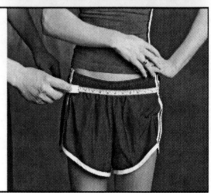

THIGHS

Stand straight up with the feet at a shoulder width stance. Evenly distribute your weight on your feet. Wrap a measuring tape around the upper thigh, just below the glutes. Do not flex the thigh muscles while measuring.

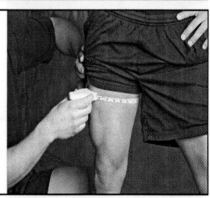

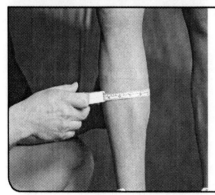

CALVES

Stand straight up with the feet at a shoulder width stance. Evenly distribute your weight on your feet. Wrap a measuring tape around the largest part of the calf muscle. Do not flex the calf muscle while measuring.

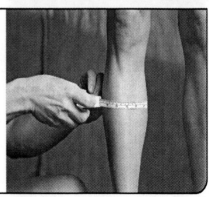

SKIN FOLD CALIPER MEASUREMENT FOR MEN

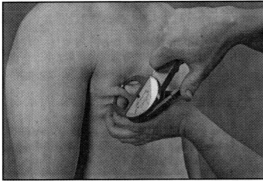

FIRST MEASUREMENT

The first measurement is taken by relaxing the muscles of the chest, pinching the skin on the right side of the chest and using the caliper to get a reading.

SECOND MEASUREMENT

The second measurement is taken by relaxing the muscles of the stomach, pinching the skin of the umbilicus or the right bottom side of the belly and using the caliper to get a reading.

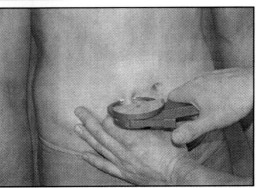

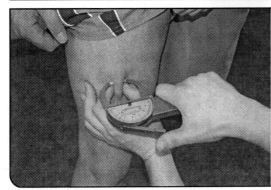

THIRD MEASUREMENT

The third measurement is taken by relaxing the muscles in the legs, pinching the skin on the outside of the mid, right thigh and using the skin fold caliper to get a reading.

SKIN FOLD CALIPER MEASUREMENT FOR WOMEN

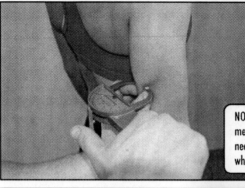

FIRST MEASUREMENT

The first measurement is taken by relaxing the muscles in the arms and having a friend pinch the back of the mid, right triceps and taking a reading.

NOTE: getting an accurate mid-triceps skin fold measurement is impossible to do by yourself. You will need the help of a friend so you can remain relaxed while the measurement is being taken.

SECOND MEASUREMENT

The second measurement is taken by relaxing the muscles around the waist and pinching a diagonal fold at a 45-degree angle just above the hip bone and getting a reading with the skin fold calipers.

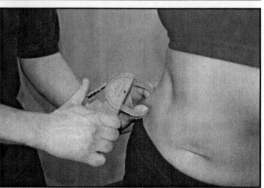

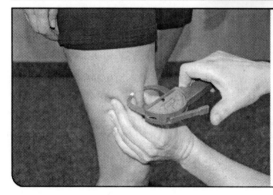

THIRD MEASUREMENT

The third measurement is taken by relaxing the muscles of the legs, pinching the skin on the outer, right mid-thigh and getting a measurement with the skin fold calipers.

Printed in the United States
69258LVS00005B/129